SARAH VAUGHAN

**Recent Titles
in Discographies**

Classical Music Discographies, 1976-1988: A Bibliography
Michael Gray, compiler

You Got To Be Original, Man!: The Music of Lester Young
Frank Büchmann-Møller

The Decca Hillbilly Discography
Cary Ginell, compiler

Percussion Discography: An International Compilation of Solo and Chamber
Percussion Music
Fernando A. Meza, compiler

TV and Studio Cast Musicals on Record: A Discography of Television Musicals
and Studio Recordings of Stage and Film Musicals
Richard Chigley Lynch, compiler

Basic Musical Library, "P" Series, 1-1000
Larry F. Kiner and Harry Mackenzie

His Master's Voice/La Voix de Son Maître
Alan Kelly, compiler

Woody Herman: A Guide to the Big Band Recordings, 1936-1987
Dexter Morrill, compiler

The Recorded Performances of Gérard Souzay: A Discography
Manuel Morris, compiler

The Aladdin/Imperial Labels: A Discography
Michel Ruppli, compiler

Rockin' the Classics and Classicizin' the Rock: A Selectively Annotated
Discography—First Supplement
Janell R. Duxbury, compiler

Igor Stravinsky—The Composer in the Recording Studio: A Comprehensive
Discography
Philip Stuart, compiler

One Night Stand Series, 1-1001
Harry Mackenzie and Lothar Polomski, compilers

Antonín Dvořák on Records
John H. Yoell, compiler

SARAH VAUGHAN

A Discography

Compiled by
DENIS BROWN

Discographies, Number 47

GREENWOOD PRESS
New York • Westport, Connecticut • London

Library of Congress Cataloging-in-Publication Data

Brown, Denis.
    Sarah Vaughan : a discography / compiled by Denis Brown.
       p. cm.—(Discographies, ISSN 0192-334X ; no. 47)
    Includes bibliographical references and index.
    ISBN 0-313-28005-3 (alk. paper)
    1. Vaughan, Sarah, 1924-   —Discography. I. Title. II. Series.
ML156.7.V4B7 1991
016.78242164'092—dc20   91-27632

British Library Cataloguing in Publication Data is available.

Copyright © 1991 by Denis Brown

Library of Congress Catalog Card Number: 91-27632
ISBN: 0-313-28005-3
ISSN: 0192-334X

First published in 1991

Greenwood Press, 88 Post Road West, Westport, CT 06881
An imprint of Greenwood Publishing Group, Inc.

Printed in the United States of America

The paper used in this book complies with the
Permanent Paper Standard issued by the National
Information Standards Organization (Z39.48-1984).

10 9 8 7 6 5 4 3 2 1

Contents

Preface

I first heard Sarah around 1950. I had been collecting
Billy Eckstine records for a few years before then, and when
I heard Sarah in a duet with him on "Dedicated To You" and
"You're All I Need," I knew that I had found my favorite
female singer.

In 1974 I completed my first discography on Dick Haymes,
a singer I had admired from the forties. This was achieved
by checking old record catalogs with all the Decca period
information from the copyright department of MCA.

When I discovered the existence of the Jepsen jazz
discographies and later the Bruyninckx one, which contained
a vast amount of information on Sarah's earliest recordings
but ended at 1960, I knew I had to work on an individual
discography of Sarah Vaughan. After ten years and three
draft versions here is my completed work, my "labor of love."

I had the great pleasure of meeting Sarah on Sunday,
November 20, 1983, at the Birmingham Odeon. Sarah was
delighted when I gave her a draft copy of the discography.
In a letter to my colleague, Mike Pearse, dated May 5, 1984,
she wrote, "I have had that book recopied about ten of them
and have put the original in my safe deposit box. Will love
it always, I just look thru that book in fact I'm doing some
tunes that I had completely forgotten about. It's like a
piece of gold, I thank you guys so much, that was so much
work and love I'm sure."

When I realised that even Sarah was unaware of many of
the songs she had recorded, I thought that her legion of fans
should be given the same opportunity to savour all of her
wonderful repetoire. I hope that you enjoy reading this
tribute as much as I enjoyed producing it.

There is still outstanding information, and I hope that
you will appreciate the difficulty in obtaining this. In many
cases the recording company has long been defunct, in others
the archivists are under commercial pressures and are unable
to find the time to do the necessary research.

The discography lists all known American and British
issues of 78s, 45s, EPs and LPs. I have also included
recordings from other countries where these were the only
versions. Four CDs are listed as I considered these to be of
particular importance. I accept the existence and excellent

sound quality of the CD; however being nostalgic and a
traditionalist I am not prepared to bow to "progress" yet.
For the benefit of CD collectors I have shown CD numbers in
the "Major Record Company's LPs" Section.

ACKNOWLEDGMENTS

     My most sincere thanks go to my fellow discographer
Ed Novitsky of Wantagh, New York, for his researching in the
Polygram archives in Edison, New Jersey, and to Dennis Drake,
who is in charge of the Polygram tape facilities, for his
generous permission to allow Ed to do this. Thanks go also to
Richard Seidel for his help, and to Kiyoshi Koyama for his
work on those wonderful boxed sets on the Japanese Mercury
label, and his kind permission to reproduce this information.
     The Roulette information was supplied by Michael Cuscuna
of New York with additional help from David Hughes of
Strategic Marketing, EMI Records (UK). I should also like to
thank Sheri Urban of Warner Records, Bernadette Moore of BMG
Music International, Martine McCarthy of CBS Records, Edwin
M. Matthias of the Library of Congress, Paul Wilson of the
National Sound Archives of the British Library and Bob Porter
for the Atlantic information.
     So many collectors have helped me that I hope a big
collective "thank you" will convey my sincere appreciation
for their assistance. I must single out Bill Miner, who
checked my drafts and made numerous corrections and
additions; Michel Ruppli for advice; and Mary M. Blair of
Greenwood Press for encouragement and assistance. Thanks to
you all. Without your help, large and small, this work
would never have reached fruition.
     Finally to "Mr. B," Billy Eckstine, who introduced me
to Sarah on the record, and to you Sassy, the Divine One,
in that great recording studio in the sky, singin' and
swingin' with the Count, Bird, Brownie, Sonny, the Duke and
all the other jazz greats: You are so greatly missed and you
will never be replaced. Thank you for all those magical
moments on stage, television and mostly on record. We will
treasure the memories for ever. You were without equal, the
ultimate talent in a multi-talented profession. God bless
you.

HOW TO USE THE DISCOGRAPHY

     The discography is divided into four sections:
I. Chronological Sessions Data; II. Song Titles and
Composers; III. Record Company Issues; and IV. Indexes of
Orchestras and Musicians.
     The first section is subdivided into three parts: The
Early Years, Mercury and Roulette and The Later Years.
Within each part, and numbered for easy reference, are listed
the individual recording sessions with information on
orchestra, musicians, where recorded and the session date(s).
The title of the orchestra may be the name of the leader or,
in the case of studio orchestras, the arranger, director or
producer. The song titles then follow in a three column
format. In the left-hand column is the matrix number or
master number. This is the number assigned to the original
production of one side of the record and is usually shown on

78s and 45s in the space (or run-out spiral) between the
record center label and the end of the playing spiral. On
45s this number is occasionally shown on the record label,
under the catalog number. In the later years, with tape
recording of the sessions, this numbering method was not
shown on the record. The second column gives the song title,
as generally known. This may have a suffix or prefix in
parenthesis. The right-hand column gives all known record
company catalog numbers in the following sequence: original
78/45, EP and LP. Following this is the British issue, minor
labels and reissues. Very minor issues may have been omitted.
        The Song Titles and Composers section serves as an index
to the previous section by cross-referencing to the number(s)
of the recording session(s) for each title. Last names of
composers are provided.
        The Record Company issues section is subdivided into
listings for LPs, Singles and EPs, and Reissues and Budget
LPs. All song titles on albums are listed.
        The final section indexes the musicians and orchestras
with reference to the recording session entry numbers.
        Using the different sections, the collector should be
able to find when a track was recorded, the name of the
orchestra and which other titles are on the record, along
with the EP or LP title.

ABBREVIATIONS

RECORD COMPANIES

Ala	Alamac	Gui	Guild	Pre	Prestige
All	Allegro	Har	Harmony	Rem	Remington
Atl	Atlantic	Hlm	Harlem Hit Parade	Riv	Riverside
Aud	Audiolab	Jaz	Jazz Anthology	Rou	Rondolette
Bir	Birchmount	Len	Lenox	Roul	Roulette
Bou	Boulevard(E)	Mas	Masterseal	Roy	Royale
Bra	Bravo(E)	Mds	Musidisc	Soc	Society(E)
Btm	Book of the Month	Merc	Mercury	Smi	Smithsonian
Bul	Bulldog(E)	MFP	Music For Pleasure(E)	Spi	Spinorama
Cam	Camay(E)	Mrs	Music Room Special	Spo	Spotlite(E)
Col	Columbia	Mur	Murray Hill	Sut	Sutton
Conc	Concord	Mus	Musicraft	Svy	Savoy
Cont	Continental	Nap	Napoleon	Swi	Swing
Cor	Coronet(E)	Pal	Palace	Tia	Tiara
Cro	Crown	Par	Parlophone(E)	Ver	Vernon
Dea	Deacon(E)	Phi	Philips(E)	Vik	Viking
Emb	Ember(E)	Pho	Phoenix	Vrv	Verve
Eve	Everest	Ply	Plymouth	Win	Windmill(E)
Ftn	Fontana(E)	Pol	Polydor(E)	WRC	World Record Club (E)
Gue	Guestar				

COUNTRIES

E	Britain	It	Italy	Sz	Switzerland
Eu	European	J	Japan		

All other recordings are of American origin

INSTRUMENTS

acc	Accordian	frh	French Horn
arr	Arranger	g	Guitar
as	Alto Sax	har	Harmonica
b	Bass	org	Organ
bar	Baritone Sax	per	Percussion
bcl	Bass Clarinet	p	Piano
bgo	Bongo	sop	Soprano Sax
bj	Banjo	synth	Synthesizer
cgs	Conga Drum	tb	Trombone
cnt	Cornet	tp	Trumpet
cond	Conductor	ts	Tenor Sax
d	Drums	tu	Tuba
elec b	Electric Bass	vbs	Vibraphone
elec g	Electric Guitar	vln	Violin
fl	Flute	vtb	Valve Trombone
flgh	Flugal Horn	vcl	Vocal
		ww	Woodwind

I
CHRONOLOGICAL
SESSIONS DATA

The Early Years

1.   BILLY ECKSTINE ORCHESTRA
Dizzy Gillespie, Shorty McConnell, Gail Brockman, Marion
Hazel (tp), Billy Eckstine (v-tb, ldr), Gerald Valentine
(tb, arr), Taswell Baird, Howard Scott, Chippy Outcalt (tb),
John Jackson, Billy Frazier (as), Dexter Gordon,
Gene Ammons (ts), Leo Parker (bar), John Malachi (p),
Connie Wainwright (g), Tommy Potter (b), Art Blakey (d).
                                     NYC, Dec 5, 1944

122   I'll Wait And   De Luxe 2003, 3003,
                 Pray   Aud AL 1549, Gue GS 1418,
                                  G 1491, (E)EMB 3338.

2.   WITH THE ALLSTARS
Dizzy Gillespie (tp), Aaron Sachs (cl), Georgie Auld (ts),
Leonard Feather (p), Chuck Wayne (g), Jack Lesberg (b),
Morey Feld (d).
                                     NYC, Dec 31, 1944

3005   Signing Off   Cont 6024, Mas M 55,
                                  Rem REP 35, RLP 1024,
                                  Pal PST 673, (E)Bul BD 1009,
                                  (E)EMB 3408.
3006   Interlude   Cont 6031, Mas M 55, Mus 33,
                                  Len 512, Rem REP 35, RLP 1024,
                                  Smi R004-P 13456, Spi CXS 215.
3007   No Smokes Blues   Cont 6061, Rem REP 35,
                 (orig. take)   RLP 1024.
3007   No Smokes Blues   Mas M 55, Mus 30 CV 1201,
                                  CV 372, Smi R004-P 13456,
                                  Spi S 73, (E)EMB 3408,
                                  (E)Chev CHV 082,
                                  (E)Par SP 601.
3008*   East Of The Sun   Cont 6031, Mas M 55, Len 512,
                                  Rem REP 35, RLP 1024,
                                  Pal PST 673, Hi-fi MS 75,
                                  Ply 12-115, (E)Bul BD 1009,
                                  (E)Chev CHV 082, (E)EMB 3408.

3007 (orig. take) The intro is on clarinet.
3007 (alt. take) The intro is on guitar, followed by trumpet.
3008* Dizzy Gillespie (p) replaces Leonard Feather.
Mas M 55 = Musicdisc CV 372, Parade SP 601, Spi S 73,
          Rem RLP 1024.
(E)Chev CHV 082 = Cor CX 277, (E) Dea 1020, (E)Win WMD 158

3.   BILLY ECKSTINE ORCHESTRA
Probably:- Gail Brockman, Marion Hazel, Shorty McConnell,
Fats Navarro (tp), Taswell Baird, Chippy Outcalt, Howard
Scott, Gerald Valentine (tb), Bill Frazier, John Jackson
(as), Gene Ammons, Budd Johnson (ts), Leo Parker (bar),
John Malachi (p), Connie Wainwright (g), Tommy Potter (b),
Art Blakey (d), Tadd Dameron (arr).
                              "Jubilee Show" LA, Feb 24, 1945

            Mean To Me   AFRS Jubilee ET 120, 216,
                                Ala QSR 2415, (E)Spo 100.

4.   BILLY ECKSTINE ORCHESTRA
Personnel Probably as Feb 24, 1945.
                              "Jubilee Show" LA, March 3, 1945

            Don't Blame Me   AFRS Jubilee ET 121, 217,
                                Ala QSR 2415, (E)Spo 100.

5.   DIZZY GILLESPIE AND HIS ALLSTAR QUINTET
Dizzy Gillespie (tp), Charlie Parker (as), Al Haigh (p),
Curley Russell (b), Sid Catlett (d).
                                       NYC, May 11, 1945

G 576-A1   Lover Man   Guild 1002, Mus 345, 499,
                               All 3080, 4006, Jax 7001,
                               Roy 1592, 1829, Even LP 399,
                               Smi P 11895, Pre P-24030,
                               Swi 317, Pho LP 2, Bell 41,
                               Eve FS 250, Ron A 853,
                               (E)Par R 3677, (E)Bra EP 305,
                               (E)Saga 6928, (E)EMB EP 4524,
                               EMB 3333, 2010.

Bell 41 = Hi-lite 41, Pickwick PR 131, Ron A 35.
Eve FS 250 = Xtra 1106, CLDE 902.

6.   DIZZY GILLESPIE AND HIS SEPTET
Dizzy Gillespie (tp), Charlie Parker (as), Flip Phillips
(ts), Nat Jaffre (p), Bill De Arango (g), Curley Russell
(b), Max Roach (d).
                                       NYC, May 25, 1945

W 3325   What More Can A   Cont 6008, LP 16004,
            Woman Do   Pal M 672, Len 500, Mus 504,
                               Metro MS 539, (E)EMB 3408,
                               (E)Spo SPJ 150.
W 3326*   I'd Rather Have A   Cont 6008, LP 16004,
            Memory Than A   Mus 504, Metro MS 539,
            Dream   (E)Spo SPJ 150.

```
W 3327      Mean To Me          Cont 6024, LP 16004, Len 500,
                                Ply P 12-146, RJ 729,
                                Hi-fi MS 75, Mas 5013, MS 33,
                                Mus 504, Metro MS 539,
                                (E)EMB 3408, (E)Spo SPJ 150.
```

W 3326* Tadd Dameron (p) replaces Jaffre.

7.   STUFF SMITH TRIO
Stuff Smith (vln), Freddy Jefferson (p), Pete Glover (d).
                                        NYC, Oct 1, 1945

```
5304        Time And Again      Mus 337, MVS 2002,
                                MGM E 3274, (E)Saga Ero 8016.
```

8.   JOHN KIRBY ORCHESTRA
Clarence Brereton (tp), Buster Bailey (cl), Russell Procope
(as), Billy Kyle (p), John Kirby (b), Bill Beason (d).
                                        NYC, Jan 9, 1946

```
BL 18       I'm Scared          Cro 107, Atl LP 116, Riv 2511.
BL 19       You Go To My Head   Cro 109, Riv 2511.
BL 20       I Can Make You       Cro 118, Riv 2511,
              Love Me
BL 21       It Might As Well     Cro 108, Atl LP 116, Riv 2511.
              Be Spring
```

Riv 2511 = Gue G 1418, Musidisc 30 CV 1201, Spi 114,
           Scepter CTN 18029, (E)London HBU 1049, REU 1065.

9.   TONY SCOTT AND HIS DOWN BEAT SEPTET
Tony Scott (as, cl), Dizzy Gillespie (tp), Trummy Young (tb),
Ben Webster (ts), Jimmy Jones (p), Gene Ramsey (b), Ed
Nicholson (d).
                                        NYC, March 6, 1946

```
S 1120      All Too Soon        Gotham 105, Atl LP 116,
                                Onyx ORI 203, (E)Pol 2344 049.
```

10.   DICKY WELLS BIG SEVEN
George Treadwell (tp), Dicky Wells (tb), Budd Johnson (ts),
Cecil Scott (bar), Jimmy Jones (p), Al McKibbon (b),
Jimmy Crawford, (d).
                                        NYC, March 21, 1946

```
1003        We're Through       HRS 1019, Alladin 3019,
                                Atl LP 116, Mus 30 CV 1201.
```

11.   GEORGIE AULD ORCHESTRA
Al Aaron, Danny Blue, Art House, Al Porcino (tp), Tracy
Allen, Mike Datz, Ruede De Luca (tb), Georgie Auld (as, ts,
ss, vcl), Lou Prisby, Gene Zanoni (as), Al Cohn, Irv Roth
(ts), Serge Chaloff (bar), Roy Kral (p), Barry Galbraith (g),
Ed Cunningham (b), Art Mardigan (d).

                                          NYC, April 30, 1946

5458	A Hundred Years From Today	Mus 458, 15072, MVS 509, All LP 1592, 3080, 3102, 4009, Bell 41, Eve FS 271, Ron A 853 MGM 30342, E 544, (E)EP 637, Lion L 70088, (E)Bra EP 305, (E)Bul BD 1009, (E)EMB 3333, 2010, (E)WRC 15, T 249.

Bell 41 = Hi-lite 41, Pickwick PR 131, Ron A 35,

12.   TADD DAMERON ORCHESTRA
Freddy Webster (tp), Leroy Harris (as), Hank Ross (b-cl),
Leo Parker (bar), 9 Strings, Budd Powell Tadd Dameron (p),
Ted Sturgis (b), Kenny Clarke (d).

                                           NYC, May 7, 1946

5485	If You Could See Me Now	Mus 380, MVS 504, MGM 11068, 30370, E 165, K 165, E 3274, (E)EP 572, Eve FS 250, Lion 70052, Metro MS 539, (E)Saga Ero 8016.
5486	I Can Make You Love Me	Mus 398, MVS 504, MGM 30341, X 1020, E 544, (E)EP 637, All LP 1608, LP 3108, Con 3018 Eve FS 325, Gue G-1591, Metro MS 539, Vik VKS-003, (E)Bou 4103, (E)Presto 678.
5487	You're Not The Kind	Mus 380, MVS 504, All LP 4006, MGM 30731, E 544, K-71, (E)EP 737, Eve FS 250, Lion 70052, 70088, Sut 239, (E)Chev CHV 082, (E)Soc 981, (E)Presto 678, (E)WRC T 249.
5488	My Kinda Love (orig. take)	Mus 398, MVS 504, MGM 30339, K-71, E 544, E 3274, (E)EP 605, All LP 1608, LP 3108, LP 4008, Conc 3018, Eve FS 250, Lion 70052, Metro MS 539, Tia TMT 7519, (E)Bra EP 305, (E)Presto 678.
5488	My Kinda Love (alt. take)	Ver 504, (E)Saga Ero 8016.

Variations on My Kinda Love takes are in the Piano fill-ins,
Baritone sax solo and the ending particularly.
Conc 3018 = (E)WRC R 3.
(E)Bou 4103 = (E)Soc 987.
(E)Chev CHV 082 = Cor CS 277, (E)DEA 1020, (E)Win WMD 158.
Eve FS 250 = Xtra 1106, CLDE 902.

13.   GEORGIE AULD ORCHESTRA
Neal Hefti, Al Porcino, Sonny Rich, George Schwartz (tp),
Mike Datz, Gus Dixon, Johnny Mandel (tb), Georgie Auld
(as, ts, sop), Gene Zanoni, Sam Zittman (as), Al Cohn, Irv
Roth (ts), Serge Chaloff (bar), Harvey Leonard (p),
Joe Pillicane (p), Art Mardigan (d).
                                      NYC, June 14, 1946

5561   You're Blase   Mus 394, 498, MVS 509,
                                    All LP 3108, Con 3018,
                                    MGM 30342, E 544, (E)EP 637,
                                    Pre 967, (E)Bul BD 1009,
                                    (E)Presto 678, (E)WRC R 3.

14.   EDDIE DAVIS QUARTET
Eddie Davis (ts, ldr), Thelonious Monk or John Lewis (p),
Ray Brown (b), Kenny Clarke (d).
                  Spotlite Club Broadcast, NYC, Prob. June, 1946

          Don't Blame Me   (Sz) Hi-fly H-01.

15.   GEORGE TREADWELL ORCHESTRA
George Treadwell (tp, ldr), Al Gibson (cl, as), George
Nicholas (ts), Eddie De Verteuil (as, bar), Jimmy Jones (p),
Jimmy Smith (g), Al McKibbon (b), William Barker (d).
                                      NYC, July 18, 1946

5613   I've Got A Crush   Mus 505, MVS 504,MGM 30339,
                 On You   X 1019, E 544, K-17, E 3274,
                                  (E)EP 605, Eve FS 325,
                                  (E)Soc 987, (E)Bou 4103.
5614   I'm Thru With   Mus 499, MVS 504, MGM 10890,
                 Love   30731, E 165, (E)EP 388,
                                  (E)EP 572, All 4041, Bell 41,
                                  Eve FS 250, Metro MS 539,
                                  Ron A 853, (E)EMB 3333, 2010.
5615   Everything I Have   Mus 494, 499, MVS 504,
                 Is Yours   All LP 1592, LP 3080, LP 4041,
                                  Bell 41, Eve FS 250,
                                  Nap NLP 11091.
5616   Body And Soul   Mus 494, MVS 504, MGM X 1020,
                                  E 544, E 3274, (E)EP 605,
                                  All LP 1608, LP 3108, LP 4009,
                                  Eve FS 250, FS 325, Roy EP 363
                                  (E)Par R 3073, (E)DGR 200,
                                  (E)Mur 927942, (E)Soc 981.

Bell 41 = Hi-lite 41, Pickwick PR 131, Ron A 35.
Eve 250 = Xtra 1106, CLDE 902.

16.   TEDDY WILSON OCTET
Buck Clayton (tp), Scoville Brown (as), Don Byas (ts), George
James (bar), Teddy Wilson (p), Remo Palmieri (g), Billy
Taylor (b), J.C.Heard (d).

NYC, Aug 19, 1946

5652	Penthouse Serenade	Mus 505, MVS 2001, All LP 3108, LP 4006, Bell 41, Con 3018, Eve FS 250, (E)Par R 3073, (E)WRC R 3.
5653	Don't Worry 'Bout Me	Mus 421, MVS 2001, MGM 30733, E 165, K-165, E 3274, (E)EP 572, All LP 3080, LP 4006, Bell 41, Eve FS 250, Lion 70052, Metro MS 539, Ron A 102, (E)Par R 3235, (E)EMB 3333, 3335, 2010,

Bell 41 = Hi-lite 41, Pickwick PR 131, Ron A 35.
Eve FS 250 = Xtra 1106, CLDE 902.

17.   TEDDY WILSON QUARTET
Charlie Ventura (ts), Teddy Wilson (p, ldr), Remo Parmieri
(g), Billy Taylor (b).

NYC, Nov 19, 1946

5809	Time After Time	Mus 462, MVS 2001, All 3080, Eve FS 271, Sut 289, 293, (E)Par R 3235, (E)Arc EP 71, (E)Presto 687.
5811	September Song	Mus 446, MVS 2001, All 3080, Bell 41, Eve FS 271, (E)Bul BD 1009, (E)EMB 3333, 2001, (E)Saga Ero 8016.

Bell 41 = Hi-lite 41, Pickwick PR 131, Ron A 35.

18.   GEORGE TREADWELL ORCHESTRA
Ermett Perry, Roger Jones, Hal Mitchell, Jesse Drakes (tp),
Ed Burke, Dick Harris, Donald Coles (tb), Rupert Cole,
Scoville Brown (as), Budd Johnson, Lowell Hastings (ts),
Eddie de Verteuill (bar), Jimmy Jones (p), Al McKibbon (b),
J.C. Heard (d).

NYC, July 2, 1947

5870	I Cover The Waterfront	Mus 503, MVS 504, MGM 10819, 30732, E 165, K-165, (E)EP 538, (E)EP 778, All LP 1608, LP 3108, Eve FS 325, (E) Presto 678, (E)Saga Ero 8016, (E)Soc 981.
5871	Ghost Of A Chance	Mus 503, MVS 504, MGM 30341, E 544, E 3274, (E)EP 605, All LP 1608, LP 3108, LP 4009, Con 3018, Ver 504, (E)Par R 3154, (E)Bou 4013, (E)Soc 987.

| 5872 | Tenderly | Mus 504, MVS 504, MGM 10705, 30730, E 165, K-165, E 3274, (E)EP 331, (E)EP 572, All LP 1608, LP 3108, LP 4041, Con 3018, Eve FS 271, Metro MS 539, Roy LP 18149, Lion 70052, (E)Bul BD 1009, (E)Presto 678, (E)Soc 981, (E)Saga Ero 8016. |
| 5873 | Don't Blame Me | Mus 504, MVS 504, MGM 11068, 30731, X 1019, E 165, K-165, E 3274, (E)EP 538, (E)EP 778, All LP 1608, LP 3108, LP 4041, Con 3018, Eve FS 325, Metro MS 539, (E)Par R 3130, (E)Soc 981. |

Con 3018 = (E)WRC R 3

19.   TED DALE ORCHESTRA
unknown strings, fhr, ww, harp.

NYC, Oct 10, 1947

5943	The Lord's Prayer	Mus 523, MVS 504, MGM 10592, All LP 1608, LP 3018, LP 4041, Con 3018, Eve FS 271, Ron A 102, Roy LP 18149, Sut 293, Tia TMT 7519, TST 519 Ver 504, (E)Bul DB 1009, (E)Saga Ero 8016, (E)Soc 981.
5944	Sometimes I Feel Like A Motherless Child	Mus 523, MVS 504, MGM 10592, All LP 1608, LP 3108, LP 4041, Con 3018, Eve FS 271, Ron A 102, Roy LP 18149, Tia TMT 7519, TST 519, Sut 293 (E)Bul BD 1009, (E)Presto 678, (E)Saga Ero 8016.
5945	I Can't Get Started omit harp, add celeste, g, b.	Mus MVS 2002, MGM 10762, Lion 70052, 70088, Ver 504, (E)Presto 678, (E)Soc 981,1001 (E)Saga Ero 8016, (E)WRC T 249
5946	Trouble Is A Man add fl.	Mus 533, MVS 2002, All LP 1592 LP 3080, LP 4041, Bell 41, Eve FS 325, Hi-lite 41, Pickwick PR 131, Ron A 37, A 102, Roy LP 18149, Vik VKS 003, (E)EMB 3333, 2010

20.   LENNIE TRISTANO QUARTET
Lennie Tristano (p, ldr), Billy Bauer (g), Tommy Potter (b), Buddy Rich (d).

"Bands For Bonds" Broadcast, NYC, Nov 8, 1947

| | Everything I Have Is Yours | (E)Spo 108, Jaz JA 5165, Zim 1002. |

21.   TED DALE ORCHESTRA
Sam Musiker (cl), unknown fhr, harp, strings, Nicholas Tagg,
(p), Tony Mottola, Al Casey (g), Mack Shopnick (b), Cozy
Cole (d), Ted Dale (arr, ldr).

NYC, Nov 8, 1947

5951	Love Me Or Leave Me	Mus 539, MVS 2006, All LP 1592 LP 3080, LP 4041, Bell 41, Eve FS 325, Ron A 853, Roy EP 363, Tia TMT 7519, TST 518, Ver 504, (E)EMB 3333, 2010.
5952	I'll Wait And Pray	Mus 586, MVS 2002, MGM 10705, (E)EP 331, Eve FS 325, Lion 70052, Sut 293, Tia TMT 7591, TST 519.
5953	I Get A Kick Out Of You	Mus 586, MVS 2002, Eve FS 325, Nap NLP 11091, (E)Soc 981.
5954	The Man I Love	Mus MVS 2002, MGM 10549, X 1020, E 165, E 3274, (E)EP 538, EP 778, Metro MS 539, Ver 504, (E)Soc 981, 1001.
5955	I'm Gonna Sit Right Down And Write Myself A Letter	Mus MVS 2002, MGM 10890, (E)EP 388, Lion 70052, Ron A 105, Sut 293, Ver 504.
5956	The One I Love Belongs To Somebody Else	Mus 552, MVS 2002, All LP 1592 LP 3080, LP 4006, Bell 41, Eve FS 271, Roy EP 221, Vik VKS 003, (E)Par R 3123, (E)Bul BD 1009, (E)EMB 3333, 2010, (E)Saga Ero 8016.
5957	Button Up Your Overcoat	Mus 593, MVS 2006, Eve FS 325, Vik VKS 003, (E)Bou 4103, (E)Soc 987.
5958	I Feel So Smoochie	Mus 533, MVS 2006,All LP 1592, LP 3080, Bell 41, Eve FS 325, Rondo RA 2005, (E)EMB 3333, 2010.
	Blue Grass	(E)Soc 981.

This track is by audition only, no positive information.
Bell 41 = Hi-lite 41, Pickwick PR 131, Ron A 35.

22.   RICHARD MALTBY STRING ORCHESTRA
unknown strings, ww, fl, harp, p, b, d.

NYC, Dec 27, 1947

6061	It's You Or No-One	Mus 557, MVS 2002, All LP 1592 LP 3080, Eve FS 271, Ron A 102 Roy EP 221, (E)Bou 4103, (E)Bul BD 1009, (E)Par R 3170.
6062	It's Magic	Mus 557, MVS 2006, All LP 1592 LP 3080, Eve FS 325, Ron A 102 Rondo RA 2005, (E)Bou 4103, (E)Par R 3170.
	I Can't Get Started	unissued

(E)Bou 4103 = (E)Soc 987.

23.   JIMMY JONES QUARTET
Jimmy Jones (p, ldr), John Collins (g), Al McKibbon (b),
Kenny Clarke (d).
                                    NYC, Dec 29, 1947

6069	What A Diff'rence A Day Made	Mus 552, MVS 2006, MGM 10762, X 1019, (E)EP 690, Con 3081, Eve FS 271, Lion 70052, 70088, (E)Par R 3130, (E)Bra EP 305, (E)Bul BD 1009, (E)Chev CHV 082, (E)Pre 678, (E)Saga Ero 8016, (E)WRC R 3.
6070	Gentleman Friend	Mus 539, MVS 2006, All LP 1592 LP 3080, Bell 41, Eve FS 271, Rondo RA 2005, (E)Bul BD 1009, (E)EMB 3333, 2010.
6071	Once In A While	Mus MVS 2002, MGM 10549, 30732 X 1020, E 165, K-165, E 3274, (E)EP 538, EP 778, Metro MS 539, (E)Bou 4103, (E)Soc 987.
6072	How Am I To Know	Soc 981.

This track is by audition only,no positive information.

Bell 41 = Hi-lite 41, Pickwick PR 131, Ron A 35.
(E)Chev CHV 082 = Cor CX 277, (E)Dea 1020, (E)Win WMD 158.

24.   EARLE RODGERS ORCHESTRA AND CHOIR
large choir, no orchestra identified by audition.
                                    NYC, April 8, 1948

| 6082 | Nature Boy | Mus 567, MVS 2006, All LP 3108 Eve FS 250, Ron A 102, (E)Bou 4103,(E)Soc 987. |
| 6083 | I'm Glad There Is You | Mus 567, All LP 1608, 3108, Ron A 102, Ver 504, (E)Bou 4103, (E)Soc 987. |

25.   JOE LIPPMAN ORCHESTRA
Gus Griffiths, Jimmy Maxwell, Red Soloman (tp), Buddy Morrow,
John D'Agostino (tb), Bernie Kaufman, Harry Terrill (as),
Hank Ross, Harold Feldman (ts), Wolffie Tannenbaum (bar),
4 violins, 1 viola, 1 cello, Bill Rowland (p), Bob Haggart
(b), Bunny Shawker (d).
                                    NYC, Jan 20, 1949

Co 40375	Bianca	Col 38461, Har HL 7158.
Co 40376	As You Desire Me	Col 38462, 50072, CL 660, CBS P 14364, Har 7158, HL 7251 HL 11318, (E)Col DB 2600, (E)Phi BBL 7082.
Co 40386	Black Coffee	Col 38462, 50072, CL 660, C2-44165, (E)Phi BBE 12094, BBL 7082, (Eu) 21114.
J 688-1118	(V-Disc matrix)	V-Disc 904-A.

26.   JOE LIPPMAN ORCHESTRA
Andy Ferretti (tp), Irving Horowitz (ts), Hyor Rosen (harp),
Terry Snyder (d), replace Griffin, Feldman, Shawker and Mills
NYC, Jan 25, 1949

Co 40426	While You Are Gone	Col 38512, CBS P 14364, C2-44165.
Co 40427	Tonight I Shall Sleep	rejected
Co 40428	That Lucky Old Sun	rejected

27.   JOE LIPPMAN ORCHESTRA
similar to Jan 20, 1949 omit saxes add fl, ww.
LA, May 6, 1949

3746	Tonight I Shall Sleep	Col 38512, CBS P 14364, Har HL 7158.
3747	That Lucky Old Sun omit tp, tb.	Col 38559, Har HL 7158, (E)Col DB 2600.

28.   HARRY SOSNICK ORCHESTRA
studio orchestra with strings and woodwinds
circa 1949

Tonight I Shall Sleep	VJC-1015-2 (CD).
While You Are Gone	VJC-1015-2 (CD).

29.   JIMMY JONES (p)
LA, Circa May,1949

Everything I Have Is Yours	(I)Kings Of Jazz KLJ 20036.
I Get A Kick Out Of You	(I)Kings Of Jazz KLJ 20036.
Tenderly	(I)Kings Of Jazz KLJ 20036.

30.   JOE LIPPMAN ORCHESTRA
Sid Cooper, Hymie Schertzer (as), Irving Horowitz, Art
Drelinger (ts), strings, Jimmy Jones (p), Al Caiola (g),
Jack Lesberg (b), Bunny Shawker (d), *unknown vocal group.
NYC, July 7, 1949

Co 40941	Give Me A Song With A Beautiful Melody	Col 38551, CBS P 14364.
Co 40942	Make Believe*	Col 38559.
Co 40943	You Taught Me To Love Again	Col 38810, B 1631, CL 660, C2-44165, (E)Phi BBE 12092, BBL 7082.
Co 40944	Just Friends	Col 38810, B 1631, CL 660, C2-44165, Har HL 11318, (E)Phi BBE 12094, BBL 7982, (Eu)CBS 21114.

31.   JIMMY JONES TRIO
Jimmy Jones (p), Joe Benjamin (b), Roy Haynes (d).
      "Just Jazz" Concert, LA Shrine Auditorium, Aug 31, 1949

            Love Me Or Leave   AFRS Just Jazz ET 58, 72,
            Me   Ozone LP 17, MRS 1006.
            Body And Soul   AFRS Just Jazz ET 58, 72,
                                Ozone LP 17,MRS 1006.

32.   HUGO WINTERHALTER ORCHESTRA
Andy Ferretti, Billy Butterfield, Jimmy Maxwell (tp), Will
Bradley, John D'Agostino, Bill Pritchard (tb), Sid Cooper,
Stan Webb (as), Hank Ross, Harold Feldman (ts), Bernie
Kaufman (bar), Jimmy Jones (p), Tony Mottola (g), Bob
Haggart (b), Terry Snyder (d).
                                      NYC, Sept 25, 1949

Co 41759   You Say You Care   rejected
Co 41760   Fool's Paradise   rejected
Co 41761   Lonely Girl   Col 38617, B 9142, CL 914,
                               (E)Phi BBL 7165.
Co 41762-1 I Cried For You   rejected

33.   SAME
                                      NYC, Sept 28, 1949

Co 41759   You Say You Care   Col 38630, Har HL 7158.
Co 41760   Fool's Paradise   Col 38617, CBS P 13517,
                               Har HL 7208.
Co 41762-2 I Cried For You   Col 38630, 5-2142, CL 660,
                               C2-44165, Har HL 11318,
                               (E)Phi PB 455, BBE 12092,
                               BBL 7082, (Eu)CBS 21114.

34.   JOE LIPPMAN ORCHESTRA
Billy Butterfield, Taft Jordon (tp), Will Bradley (tb), Toots
Mondello, Hymie Schertzer (as), Art Drelinger, George Kelly
(ts), Stan Webb (bar), Jimmy Jones (p), Al Caiola (g),
Eddie Safranski (b), Cozy Cole (d).
                                      NYC, Dec 21, 1949

Co 42530   You're Mine You   Col 39071, 500046, 5-2143,
                               CL 660, 2C-44165,
                               (E)Phi BBE 12092, BBL 7082.
Co 42531   I'm Crazy To Love   Col 38701, B 9143, CL 914,
           You   2C-44165, (E)Phi BBL 7165.
Co 42532   Summertime   Col 38701, 5-2142, Cl 660,
                               2C-44165, Har HL 11318,
                               (E)Phi PB 455, BBE 12094,
                               BBL 7082, (Eu) CBS 21114.
Co 42533   The Nearness Of   Col 39071, 500046, B 7451,
           You   CL 745, 2C-44165,
                               (E)Phi BBE 12036, BBL 7082,
                               (Eu)CBS 21114.

35.   JOE LIPPMAN ORCHESTRA, DUET WITH BILLY ECKSTINE (vcl)
Toots Mondello, Bernie Kaufman (cl, fl), Art Drelinger, Hank
Ross (cl, b-cl, ts), unknown strings, Jimmy Jones (p),
Sid Weiss (b), Bunny Shawker (d).

NYC, Dec 22, 1949

49 S 428	Ev'ry Day	MGM 11144, X 1002, (E)EP 561, Lion L 70088, Vrv 819 442-1, (E)WRC T 249.
49 S 429	I Love You	MGM 11144, X 1002, (E)EP 561, Lion 70088, Vrv 819 442-1, (E)WRC T 249.
49 S 430	Dedicated To You	MGM 10690, X 1002, (E) 308, (E)EP 561, Lion L 7008, Vrv MGV (S6) 8505, 819 4442-1 (E)MFP 5244, (E)WRC T 249.
49 S 331	You're All I Need	MGM 10690, 45-8005, X 1002, (E) 308, EP 561, Lion L 7008, Vrv 819 442-1, (E)MFP 4233, (E)WRC T 249.

36.   JIMMY JONES (p)

Concert, Carnegie Hall, NYC, Dec 25, 1949

Once In A While	V.O.A ET, IAJRC LP 20.
Mean To Me	V.O.A.ET, IAJRC LP 20.

Both ex-Voice of America ET's

37.   NORMAN LEYDEN ORCHESTRA
Bob Cusamano, John Carroll, Bernie Privin (tp), Jack
Satterfield, John D'Agostino (tb), Bill Versaci ,Paul Ricci,
Tom Parshley, Harry Terrill, G. Tudor (saxes), Bernie
Leighton (p), Frank Carroll (b), Terry Snyder (d).

NYC, May 4, 1950

Co 43209	Our Very Own	Col 38860, Har HL 7208.
Co 43210	Don't Be Afraid	Col 38861, B 9143, CL 914, (E)Phi BBL 7165.

38.   GEORGE TREADWELL AND HIS ALLSTARS
Miles Davis (tp), Benny Green (tb), Tony Scott (cl), Budd
Johnson (ts), Jimmy Jones (p), Freddie Green (g), Billy
Taylor (b), J.C.Heard (d).

NYC, May 18, 1950

Co 43825	Ain't Misbehavin'	Col 38896, CL 745, CL 6133, 2C-44165, Har HL 7125, (E)Col D 600, (E)CBS 54303, 67203, (Eu)CBS 21114.
Co 43826	Goodnight My Love	Col 38897, CL 745, CL 6133, 2C-44165, Har HL 7125, (E)Col D 600, (E)CBS 54303, (Eu)CBS 21114.
Co 43827	Can't Get Out Of This Mood	Col 38898, CL 745, CL 6133, 2C-44165, (Eu)CBS 21114.
Co 43828	It Might As Well Be Spring	Col 38899, CL 745, CL 6133, 2C-44165, (Eu)CBS 21114.

39.   SAME
Mundell Lowe (elect g), replaces Green.

NYC, May 19, 1950

Co 43829-?	Mean To Me (orig. take)	Col 38899, CL 6133, 2C-44165, (Eu)CBS 21114.
Co 43829-?	Mean To Me (alt. take)	Col CL 745.
Co 43830	Come Rain Or Come Shine	Col 38898, CL 745, CL 6133, 2C-44165, Har HL 11318, (E)Phi BBL 7082, BBE 12036 (Eu)CBS 21114.
Co 43831	Nice Work If You Can Get It	Col 38897, CL 745, CL 6133, CBS P 14364, 2C-44165, Har HL 7125, (E)Phi BBL 7082, BBE 12036, (E)CBS 66413, (Eu)CBS 21114.
Co 43832	East Of The Sun	Col 38896, CL 745, CL 6133, CBS P 14364, 2C-44165, Har HL 11318, (E)CBS 54303, (Eu)CBS 21114.

40.   NORMAN LEYDEN ORCHESTRA
Red Solomon, Gus Griffith, Jimmy Maxwell (tp), Buddy Morrow,
Will Bradley, Jack Satterfield (tb), Bill Versaci, Al Klink,
Jimmy Abato, Russ Banzer, Jimmy Odriche (saxes), Bud Powell
(p), Mundell Lowe (g), Frank Carroll (b), Terry Snyder (d).

NYC July 27, 1950

Co 44130	I Love The Guy	Col 38925.
Co 44131	Thinking Of You	Col 38925, CL 660, C2-44165, (E)DB 2771, (Eu)CBS 21114.

41.   STAN GETZ BAND
Stan Fishelson, Al Porcino, Idris Sulieman (tp), Johnny
Mandel (bass tb), Stan Getz, Zoot Sims (ts), Gerry Mulligan
(bar), Billy Taylor (p), Tommy Potter (b), Roy Haynes (d).

Live, Apollo Theatre, NYC, Aug 17, 1950

My Gentleman Friend Charlie Parker Records CP 503.
You're All Need   Charlie Parker Records CP 503.

This recording was made from the house PA system, with a
cassette recorder,in the dressing room.

42.   CHARLIE PARKER QUARTET
Charlie Parker (as), Al Haigh or Bernie Leighton (p), Tommy
Potter (b), Roy Haynes (d).

NYC, Aug 17-24, 1950

I Cried For You   (E)Saga Ero 8006.

This recording is reputed to exist, but there is no
authentication to date.

43.   NORMAN LEYDEN ORCHESTRA
As July 27, 1950 except John Fulton (sax), Stan Freeman (p),
replace Klink and Powell. Bradley (tb) out.
                                            NYC, Sept 5, 1950

Co 44308   Whippa-Whippa-Woo   unissued
Co 44309   Perdido   Col 39001, CL 660, CL 777,
                               C2-44165, (Eu)CBS 21114.

44.   SAME
                                            NYC, Sept 7, 1950

Co 44308   Whippa-Whippa-Woo   Col 39001, Har HL 7208.

45.   NORMAN LEYDEN ORCHESTRA
Bernie Privin, Yank Lawson, Carl Poole (tp), Will Bradley,
Jack Satterfield, Bill Rausch (tb), Bill Versaci, Al Klink,
Russ Banzer, Jim Abato, Bill Hitz (saxes), Jimmy Jones (p),
Mundell Lowe (g), Frank Carroll (b), Bunny Shawker (d), Joe
Lewis Mangual (bgo).
                                            NYC, Dec 6, 1950

Co 44700   I'll Know   Col 39124, CBS P 13517,
                               C2-44165, Har HL 7208.
Co 44701   De Gas Pipe She's   Col 39124, CBS P 13517,
             Leakin' Joe   Har HL 7208.

46.   NORMAN LEYDEN ORCHESTRA
10 Strings, Billy Taylor (chimes), Frank Carroll (b).
                                            NYC, Jan 17, 1951

Co 45114   Ave Maria   Col 39207, CBS P 13517,
                               Har HL 7208, AFRS 25.
Co 45115   A City Called   Col 39207, CBS P 13517,
             Heaven   Har HL 7208, AFRS 25.

47.   PERCY FAITH ORCHESTRA
Jim Abato, Bernie Kaufman, Al Freistat, Russ Banzer, E Brown,
(woodwinds), 6 violins, 1 viola, 1 cello, Stan Freeman (p),
Art Ryerson (g), Frank Carroll (b), Terry Snyder (d).
                                            NYC, April 4, 1950

Co 45191   Deep Purple   Col 39370, B 1631, B 2551,
                               CL 660, C2-44165, Har HL 11318
Co 45192   These Things I   Col 39370, B 9141, CL 914,
             Offer You   CBS P 14364, (E)Phi BBL 7165.
           Vanity   rejected.
           My Reverie   rejected.

48.   PAUL WESTON ORCHESTRA
Ziggy Elman, Zeke Zarchy, Frank Fletcher-Beach (tp), Bill
Schaefer, Allan Thompson, Elmer Smithers (tb), Fred Stulce,
Harold Lawson, Don Lodice, Babe Russin, Leonard Harman
(saxes), Milt Raskin (p), George Van Eps (g), John Ryan (b),
Nick Fatool (d).
                                    Hollywood, June 1, 1951

RHCO 4499   Vanity   Col 39446, CBS P 13517,
                                Har HL 7208.
RHCO 4500   My Revie   Col 39446, B 42143, CL 660,
                                C2-44165.
RHCO 4501   Out Of Breath   Col 39494.
RHCO 4502   After Hours   Col 39494, 5-2142, CL 660,
                                C2-44165, AFRS 25.

49.   WITH HER TRIO
Probably Jimmy Jones (p), Joe Benjamin (b), Roy Haynes (d).
                              Ann Arbor, Michigan, Nov 15, 1951

          I Ran All The Way   VJC-1015-2 (CD).
          Home

50.   DUKE ELLINGTON ORCHESTRA DUET WITH NAT KING COLE (vcl)*
Probably Clark Terry, Willie Cook, Francis Williams, Ray
Nance, Dick Vance (tp), Juan Tizol, Britt Woodman, Quentin
Jackson (tb), Jimmy Hamilton, Russell Procope, Willie Smith,
Paul Gonsalves, Harry Carney (reeds), Jimmy Jones (p),
Joe Benjamin (b), Roy Haynes (d), Duke Ellington (arr, cond).
                              Ann Arbor, Michigan, Nov 15, 1951

          Mean To Me (incomp) VJC-1015-2 (CD).
          Perdido   VJC-1015-2 (CD).
          Love You Madly*   VJC-1015-2 (CD).

51.   PERCY FAITH ORCHESTRA
Toots Mondello, Jim Abato, Al Freistat, Russ Banzer, Harold
Feldman (saxes), 5 violins, 2 viola, 1 cello, Stan Freeman
(p), Art Ryerson (g), Frank Carroll (b), Phil Kraus (d, vib).
                                      NYC, Sept 19, 1951

Co 47068   Just A Moment More Col 39576, B 9142, CL 914,
                               (E)Phi BBL 7165.
Co 47069   Pinky   Col 39634, B 7451, CL 745,
                               KL 5141, C2-44165,
                               (Eu)CBS 21114.
Co 47070   I Ran All The Way   Col 39576, CBS P 13517,
           Home   Har HL 7208.
Co 47071   A Miracle Happened Col 39634, CBS P 14364,
                               Har HL 7158.

52.   PERCY FAITH ORCHESTRA
Jack Satterfield, L Altpeter, Al Godlis (tb),Toots Mondello,
Al Freistat, Bill Versaci, Russ Banzer, Paul Ricci (saxes),
5 violins, 2 viola, 1 cello, Bob Kitsis (p), Art Ryerson (g),
Frank Carroll (b), Phil Kraus (d).

                                          NYC, March 19, 1952

Co 47381	Street Of Dreams	Col 39789, B 1631, B 2551, CL 660, C2-44165.
Co 47382	Time To Go	Col 39789, CBS P 13517, Har HL 7208, AFRS 25.
Co 47383	Corner To Corner	Col 39719, CBS P 13517, Har HL 7208, (E)Col DB 576.
Co 47384	If Someone Had Told Me	Col 39719, CBS P 14364, Har HL 7158, (E)Col DB 576.

53.   WITH HER TRIO PLUS GUEST
Probably Lou Stein (p), Al Hall or Joe Benjamin (b), unknown
drums, with Wild Bill Davis* (org), added guest
                         Broadcast, Birdland, NYC, March 22, 1952

Vanity	Alto AL 712, MRS 5024.
Mean To Me	Alto AL 712, MRS 5024.
Tenderly	Alto Al 712, MRS 5024.
Perdido*	Alto AL 712, MRS 5024.
Once In A While	Alto AL 712, MRS 5024.

54.   PERCY FAITH ORCHESTRA
Gus Griffith, Red Solomon, J Milazzo (tp), L Altpeter,
R Dupont, John D'Agostino (tb), Bernie Kaufman, Al Freistat,
Bill Versaci, T Gompers, Harold Freeman (saxes), unknown
strings, Lou Stein (p), Art Ryerson (g), Frank Carroll (b),
Terry Snyder (d).

                                          NYC, July 28, 1952

Co 48127	Say You'll Wait For Me	Col 39839, CBS P 13517, Har HL 7208, (E)Col DB 3172.
Co 48128	Sinner Or Saint	Col 39873, B 9142, CL 914, CL 6233, (E)Col DB 3197, (E)Phi BBR 8115.
Co 48129	My Tormented Heart	Col 39839, B 9142, CL 914, CL 6233, (E)Col DB 3172.
Co 48130	Mighty Lonesome Feeling	Col 39873, B 9143, CL 914, (E)Col DB 3197.

55.   WITH HER TRIO
personnel not known
                         Broadcast, Birdland, NYC, Aug 23, 1952

Once In A While	Alto AL 712, MRS 5024.
I Cried For You	Alto AL 712, MRS 5024.
Street Of Dreams	Alto AL 712, MRS 5024, 5037.
Perdido	Alto AL 712, MRS 5024.
I Ran All The Way Home	Alto AL 712, MRS 5024.
Time To Go	Alto AL 712, MRS 5024.

56.   PERCY FAITH ORCHESTRA
Will Bradley, Jack Satterfield, Al Godlis (tb), 5 violins,
2 viola, Lou Stein (p), Art Ryerson (g), Frank Carroll (b),
Terry Snyder (d).
                                          NYC, Dec 30, 1952

Co 48723-1 I Confess   Col 39932, B 9141, CL 914.
Co 48724-1 Lover's Quarrel   Col 39932, B 9141, CL 914.
Co 48725   Time   Col 40041, Har HL 7158,
                              (E)Phi BBR 8115.

57.   PERCY FAITH ORCHESTRA
As Dec 30, 1952 , with Red Solomon, Jimmy Maxwell, J Milozzo,
P Cincillo (tp), Bernie Kaufman, Jim Abato, Bill Versaci,
Harold Freeman, Russ Banzer (saxes) added.
                                           NYC, Jan 5, 1953

Co 48728   Linger Awhile   Col 40041, B 9141, CL 914,
                              CBS P 14364, Har HL 11318,
                              (E)Phi BBL 7082, BBE 12094.
Co 48729-1 Spring Will Be A   Col 39963, B 7453, CL 745,
           Little Late This   C2-44165.
           Year
Co 48730-1 A Blues Serenade   Col 39963, B 9143, CL 914,
                              C2-44165.
Co 48732   Ooh, Watcha Doin' Col B 7453, CL 745, C2-44165,
            To Me   (E)Phi BBL 7082, BBE 12036,
                              (Eu)CBS 21114.

58.   DIZZY GILLESPIE QUINTET
Dizzy Gillespie (tp), Bill Graham (bar), Wade Legge (p),
Lou Hackney (b), Al Jones (d).
                    Concert, Salle Pleyel, Paris, Feb 9, 1953

           Embraceable You   (I)Europa Jazz EJ 1002,
                              (I)I Grande Del Jazz GJ-2.

59.   UNKNOWN PIANO ACCOMPANIMENT
                    Broadcast, Apollo Theatre, NYC, April 29, 1953

           Street Of Dreams   Session SR 124.

60.   WITH HER TRIO
John Malachi (p), Joe Benjamin (b), Roy Haynes (d).
                    Broadcast, Birdland, NYC, Sept 5, 1953

                Body And Soul   Alto AL 712, MRS 5024.
                Nice Work If You   Alto AL 712, MRS 5024.
                  Can Get It
                Everything I Have Alto AL 712, MRS 5024.
                  Is Yours
                Summertime   Alto AL 712, MRS 5024.
                Linger Awhile   Alto AL 712, MRS 5024.
                East Of The Sun   Alto AL 712, MRS 5024.

61.   UNIDENTIFIED BIG BAND
possibly 5 tp, 5 tb, 5 saxes, p, g, b, d.

                                       Probably circa 1951-53

          You're Mine You   (E)Win WMD 158.
          The Nearness Of You (E)Win WMD 158.
          You're Not The Kind (E)Win WMD 158.
          These Things I   (E)Win WMD 158.
            Offer You
          Perdido   (E)Win WMD 158.

(E)Win WMD 158 = (E)Camay CA 3041, (E)Chev CHV 082,
                 (E)Cor CX 277, (E)Dea DEA 1020.

62.   BOB SIMMENS GROUP
                        Broadcast, NYC, Probably circa 1953

          For You   AFRS 1552.
          Bianca   AFRS 1552.
          As You Desire Me   AFRS 1552.
          Body And Soul   AFRS 1552.
          I Cried For You   AFRS 1552.

These tracks may possibly be commercial recordings played
by a presenter, although this does not explain the first
track, which has not been issued commercially.

Mercury And Roulette

63.   RICHARD HAYMAN ORCHESTRA
                                              NYC, Feb 10, 1954

10114-8	I Still Believe In You	Merc MG 20540.
10115-3	My Funny Valentine	Merc EP1-3232, Wing MGW 12123 SRW 16123, (E)Wing WL 1083, Hlm HHP 8003, (E) WRC TP 230, (E) Merc 824 864-1.
10116-2	My One And Only Love	Merc MG 20219.
10117-3	Come Along With Me	Merc 70331, MG 20540.

64.   DON COSTA ORCHESTRA
                                              NYC, March 29, 1954

10283	Imagination	Merc EP1-3232, MG 20540.
10284	It's Easy To Remember	Merc 70331, EP1-3232, MG 20219, (E) 842 864-1.
10285	And This Is My Beloved	Merc 70299, MG 20219, (E) MB 3210.
10286	Easy Come,Easy Go Lover	Merc 70299, EP-3232, Wing MGW 12123,SRW 16123, (E) WRC TP 230.

65.   WITH HER TRIO
John Malachi (p), Joe Benjamin (b), Roy Haynes (d).
                                              NYC, April 2, 1954

10413	Lover Man	EmArcy EP1-6001, MG 36109.
10414	Shulie A Bop	EmArcy 16005, EP1-6001, MG 36071, MG 36109, (E) MB 3129, (E) EJL 1277.
10415	Polka Dots And Moonbeams	EmArcy 16005, EP1-6001, MG 36109.
10416	Body And Soul	EmArcy EP1-6001, MG 36109.
10417	They Can't Take Away From Me	EmArcy EP1-6000, MG 36109, (E) ep1-600.
10418	Prelude To A Kiss	EmArcy EP1-6000, MG 36109, (E) ep1-600.

| 10419 | You Hit The Spot | EmArcy EP1-6000, MG 36109, (E) ep1-600. |
| 10420 | If I Knew Then | EmArcy EP1-6000, MG 36109, (E) ep1-600. |

MG 36109 = MG 26005, (E) EJL 1273, (E) MPT 7518*,
         (E) 6336 713, Trip TLP 5551.
* Except "You Hit The Spot"
10114 - 10286 and 10418 - 10420 on (J) 18PJ-1030

66.   HUGO PERETTI ORCHESTRA
                                    NYC, July 6, 1954

10586	Old Love	Merc Wing MGW 12123.
10587	Old Devil Moon	Merc 70423, EP1-3287, MG 20219.
10588	Exactly Like You	Merc MG 20223, (E) MPT 6540.
10589	Saturday	Merc 70423, EP1-3287, Wing MGW 12123, SRW 16123, (E) WRC TP 230.

67.   HUGO PERETTI ORCHESTRA
                                    NYC, Sept 24, 1954

10742	Only Love Me	unissued
10743	When You're In Love	unissued
10744	Idle Gossip	Merc 70469, EP-3287, MG 20219, (E) MLP 6532, Bir BM 687.
10745	Make Yourself Comfortable	Merc 70469, EP1-3287, MG 20094, MG 20645, MGD 25205, (E)MPT 7503, (E)SMWL 21045, Bir BM 687.

68.   COUNT BASIE BAND PLUS HER TRIO
Thad Jones, Reunald Jones, Wendell Culley, Joe Newman (tp),
Bill Hughes, Henry Coker, Benny Powell (tb), Marshall Royal
(as, cl), Ernie Wilkins (ts), Frank Wess (ts, fl), Frank
Foster (ts), Charlie Fowlkes (bar), (minus Basie and rhythm)
Jimmy Jones (p), Joe Benjamin (b), Roy Haynes (d).
                 Carnegie Hall Concert, NYC, Sept 25, 1954

	Perdido*	Roul RE 127.
	Polka Dots And Moonbeams +	Roul RE 127.
Medley;-	I Ain't Mad At You*+	Roul RE 127.
	Summertime *+	
	Saturday +	Roul RE 127.
	Time +	Roul RE 127.
	Old Devil Moon*	Roul RE 127.
	Tenderly +	Roul RE 127.
	Don't Blame Me +	Roul RE 127.

*+ With Trio and Band   * With Basie Band   + With Trio
Roulette RE 127 = Vogue SLVSXR 681

69.   HUGO PERETTI ORCHESTRA
                                    NYC, Oct 20-21, 1954

10794   Oh,Yeah   Merc 70595, EP1-4017,
                                 MG 20219, MGD 25219,
                                 (E) MPL 6532.
10795-1   I'm In The Mood   Merc EP1-3305, MG 20094,
            For Love   MG 25213, (E) MPT 7503.
10796-1   I Don't Know Why   Merc EP1-3305, MG 20094,
                                 (E) MPT 7503.
10798-4   Let's Put Out The   Merc EP1-3305, MG 20094,
            Lights And Go   MG 25213, (E) MPT 7503.
            To Sleep
10799   Waltzing Down The   Merc 70534, EP1-4017,
            Aisle   MG 20223, (E) MB 3210,
                                 (E) MLP 6540.
10800-1   It's Magic   Merc EP1-3304, MG 20094,
                                 MG 25213, (E) ZEP 10054,
                                 (E) MPT 7503.
10801-1   Honey   Merc EP1-3305, MG 20094,
                                 MG 25213, (E) MPT 7503.

70.   HUGO PERETTI ORCHESTRA
                                    NYC, Circa Nov/Dec, 1954

10811   How Important Can   Merc 70554, EP1-4017,
            It Be   MG 20223, MG 20645, SR 60645,
                                 Bir BM 687.
10814-3   The Touch Of Your   Merc EP1-3304, MG 20094,
            Lips   MG 25213, (E) MPT 7503.
10815-5   'S Wonderful   Merc EP1-3304, MG 20094,
                                 MG 25213, (E) ZEP 10054,
                                 (E) MPT 7503.
10816-1   Tenderly   Merc EP-1 3304, MG 20094,
                                 MG 25213, (E) MPT 7503.

10586 - 10745 and 10794 - 10816 on (J) 18PJ 1031.

71.   COUNT BASIE BAND PLUS HER TRIO
Personnel As Sept 25, 1954
                        Live, Birdland NYC, Circa Dec 16, 1954

            'S Wonderful*   Roul RE 126.
            It's Easy To   Roul RE 126.
            Remember*
            East Of The Sun*   Roul RE 126.
            How Important Can   Roul RE 126.
            It Be*
            Old Devil Moon*   Roul RE 126.
            Make Yourself   Roul RE 126.
            Comfortable*+
            SV Closing Announcement

72.   ERNIE WILKINS ORCHESTRA
Clifford Brown (tp), Herbie Mann (fl), Paul Quinichette (ts),
Jimmy Jones (p), Joe Benjamin (b), Roy Haynes (d),Ernie
Wilkins (arr. dir).

                                        NYC, Dec 16, 1954

11077-8	September Song	EmArcy EP1-6099, MG 36004, (E) Phi Sonic 031.
11078	Lullaby Of Birdland	EmArcy EP1-6099, MG 20645, MG 36004, MG 36087, C 30031, Bir BM 687.
11079-6	I'm Glad There is You	EmArcy EP1-6098, MG 36004.
11080-7	You're Not The Kind	EmArcy EP1-6097,MG 36004, (E) EJL 1250.

73.   ERNIE WILKINS ORCHESTRA
Personnel As Dec 16, 1954

                                        NYC, Dec 18, 1954

11081-5	Jim	EmArcy EP1-6096, MG 36004, (E) YEP 9507.
11082-5	He's My Guy	EmArcy EP1-6096,MG 36004, (E) 20109 SMCL.
11083-8	April In Paris	EmArcy EP1-6097, MG 36004, (E) YEP 9507.
11084-4	It's Crazy	EmArcy MG 36004.
11085-1	Embraceable You	EmArcy EP1-6098, MG 36004, (E) 6612 056.

MG 36004 = (E) 20055 MCL, (E) MCL 125061, (E) 6336 32918,
           (E) 6336 705, Trip TLP 5501 And (J) 18PJ-1032.

74.   COUNT BASIE ORCHESTRA
Wendell Culley, Reunald Jones, Thad Jones, Joe Newman (tp),
Henry Coker, Bill Hughes, Benny Powell (tb), Marshall Royal
(cl, as), Bill Graham (as), Frank Wess (fl, ts),Frank Foster
(ts), Charlie Fowlkes (bar), Freddie Green (g), Jimmy Jones
(arr, p), Joe Benjamin (b), Roy Haynes (d).
                  Municipal Auditorium, Topeka, Kansas, Feb, 1955

'S Wonderful	Jass J-CD-17.
It's Easy To Remember	Jass J-CD-17.
East Of The Sun	Jass J-CD-17.
How Important Can It Be	Jass J-CD-17.
Old Devil Moon	Jass J-CD-17.
Idle Gossip	Jass J-CD-17.
Make Yourself Comfortable	Jass J-CD-17.
Perdido	Jass J-CB-17.

75.   HUGO PERETTI ORCHESTRA
                                    NYC, March 17, 1955

11265   Whatever Lola   Merc 70595, 3324, EP1-4017,
               Wants   MG 20219, MG 20645, MGD 25217,
                                    SR 60645, (E)MT 751,
                                    (E)MEP 9509, (E)MEP 9511,
                                    (E) MPL 6532, Bir MB 687.

76.   HUGO PERETTI ORCHESTRA
                                    NYC, March 20, 1955

11297   Slowly With   Merc 70646, MG 20223,
               Feeling   (E) MPL 6540.
11298   Experience   Merc 70646, MG 20219,
               Unnecessary   (E) MPL 6532.

77.   HUGO PERETTI ORCHESTRA
                                    NYC, Aug 9, 1955

11664   Fabulous Character   Merc 70885, MG 20223,
                                    (E) MT 123.
11665   Johnny Be Smart   Merc 70693, EP1-4018,
                                    MG 20219, (E) MPL 6532.
11666   Hey Naughty Papa   Merc 70693, Wing MGW 12237.

78.   HUGO PERETTI ORCHESTRA
                                    NYC, Oct 10, 1955

11749   The Other Woman   Merc 70885, MG 20219,
                                    (E) MT 133, (E) MPL 6632,
                                    (E) MPT 7506.
11750-14   Never   Merc (J).
11750-16   Never   Merc 70727, MG 20223,
                                    (E) MPL 6540.
11751-1   C'est La Vie   Merc (J).
11751-6   C'est La Vie   Merc 70727, EP1-4019,
                                    MG 20223, (E) YEP 9511,
                                    (E) MPL 6540.

79.   HUGO PERETTI ORCHESTRA
                                    NYC, Circa Mid Oct, 1955

12129-3   Paradise   Merc MG 20094, (E)MPT 7503,
12130-1   Time On My Hands   Merc (J).
12130-3   Time On My Hands   Merc MG 20094, (E)MPT 7503.
12131-3   Gimme A Little   Merc MG 20094, (E)MPT 7503.
               Kiss

80.   HUGO PERRETTI ORCHESTRA
                                    NYC, Oct 22, 1955

12260   Mr. Wonderful   Merc 70777, EP1-4021, MG 20219
                                    (E)MEP 9511, (E)MPT 7523.
12261   You Ought To Have   Merc 70777, MG 20223,
               A Wife   (E)MPT 6540.

81.   ERNIE WILKINS ORCHESTRA
Ernie Royal, Bernie Glow (tp), J.J.Johnson, Kai Winding (tb),
Julian (Cannonball) Adderley, Sam Marowitz (as), Jerome
Richardson (fl, ts), Jimmy Jones (p), Turk Van Lake (g),
Joe Benjamin (b), Roy Haynes (d).

                                   NYC, Oct 25, 1955

12266-1   Sometimes I'm Happy   Merc (J).
12266-2   Sometimes I'm Happy   Merc (J).
12266-3   Sometimes I'm Happy   Merc (J).
12266-4   Sometimes I'm Happy   EmArcy MG 36058, MG 20133,
                                   (E)Ema ERE 1550.
12267-1   I'll Never Smile   Merc (J).
             Again
12267-2   I'll Never Smile   Merc (J).
             Again
12267-3   I'll Never Smile   EmArcy MG 36058, (E)EP1-6147.
             Again
12268-3   Don't Be On The   Merc (J).
             Outside
12268-5   Don't Be On The   EmArcy MG 36058, 6147,
             Outside   (E)Ema ERE 1550.
12269   It Shouldn't   EmArcy 70086, MG 36058,
             Happen To A Dream   MG 36086.

11265 - 12266 on Merc (J) 18PJ-1033.

82.   ERNIE WILKINS ORCHESTRA

Personnel as Oct 25, 1955.
                                   NYC, Oct 26, 1955

12270   An Occasional Man   EmArcy MG 36058, EP1-6519.
12271   Soon   EmArcy MG 36058, (E) 6619 035.
12272   Cherokee   EmArcy MG 36058,
                                   (E)Ema ERE 1550.
12273   Maybe   EmArcy MG 36058, EP1-6520.

83.   ERNIE WILKINS ORCHESTRA
Personnel as Oct 25, 1955.
                                   NYC, Oct 27, 1955

12278   Why Can't I?   EmArcy MG 36058, 824 864-1.
12279   How High The Moon?   EmArcy MG 36058, (E)EP1-6147,
                                   (E)Ema ERE 1550.
12280-1   Over The Rainbow   Merc (J).
12280-3   Over The Rainbow   Merc 70086, 6147,
                                   EmArcy MG 36058, MG 36086.
12281-2   Oh, My   Merc (J).
12281-6   Oh, My   Merc (J).
12281-8   Oh, My   EmArcy MG 36058.

MG 36058 = Merc (E)EJL 100, Trip TLP 5523.
12267 - 12281 on Merc (J) 18PJ-1034.

84.   HAL MOONEY ORCHESTRA
                                    NYC, April 1, 1956

12596   The Boy Next Door   EmArcy MG 36089,
                              Wing MGW 12237,
                              (E)Wing WL 1083.
12597   Shake Down The   EmArcy MG 36089, 2-6163,
         Stars   Wing MGW 12237,
                              (E)Wing WL 1083.
12598   The Masquerade   EmArcy MG 36089, 2-6163,
         Is Over   Wing MGW 12237,
                              (E)Wing WL 1083, Hlm HHP 8003.
12599   Lush Life   EmArcy MG 36088, MG 36089,
                              2-6163, Wing MGW 12237,
                              (E)Wing WL 1083,
                              (E)Phi Sonic 031.
12600   A Sinner Kissed   EmArcy MG 36089, 2-6163,
         An Angel   Wing MGW 12237,
             .   (E)Wing WL 1083,
                              (E)Phi Sonic 031.
12601   Old Folks   EmArcy MG 36089.
12602   The House I Live   Merc MG 20617, SR 60617,
         In   (E)20042 SMCL.
12603   I'm The Girl   EmArcy MG 36088, 2-6163.

MG 36089 = Merc (E)EJL 1258, Trip TLP 5517.

85.   HAL MOONEY ORCHESTRA
                                    NYC, April 2, 1956

12833-7   Hot And Cold   Merc 70846, MG 20540, SR 60225
          Running Tears
12834-10 The Edge Of The Sea Merc MG 20223, (E)MPT 6540.
12835-3   I've Got Some   EmArcy MG 36089, 2-6163,
          Crying To Do   Wing MGW 12237,
                              (E)Wing WL 1083.
12836-5   That's Not The   Merc 70846, MG 20540, SR 60225
          Kind Of Love

86.   HAL MOONEY ORCHESTRA
                                    NYC, April 8, 1956

12842   My Romance   EmArcy MG 36089, 2-6163,
                              824 864-1.
12843   Lonely Woman   EmArcy MG 36089, 2-6163.
12844   Only You Can Say   EmArcy MG 36089,
                              Wing MGW 12237,
                              (E)Wing WL 1083.
12845   I Loved Him   EmArcy MG 36089.

MG 36089 = Merc (E)EJL 1258, Trip TLP 5517.

87.   HUGO PERETTI ORCHESTRA

NYC, June 21, 1956

13349-8	It Happened Again	Merc 70947, MG 20223, (E)MPL 6540.
13350-12	I Wanna Play House	Merc 70947, MG 20219, (E)MPL 6532.

12596 - 13350 on Merc (J) 18PJ-1035.

88.   HAL MOONEY ORCHESTRA

NYC, Oct 29, 1956

14413	You're My Everything	Merc (J).
14414	Autumn In New York	Merc MG 20244, MG 20645, BM 687.
14415	My Darling, My Darling	Merc 20244, (E)MT 198.
14416	Little Girl Blue	Merc MG 20244, 824 864-1.
14417	Bewitched	Merc MG 20244, 824 864-1, (E)MT 198.
14418	Dancing In The Dark	Merc 20245, Smi P-11895.

89.   HAL MOONEY ORCHESTRA

NYC, Oct 30, 1956

14423-5	Can't We Be Friends	Merc (J).
14424	All The Things You Are	Merc MG 20245, (E) 6199 035.
14425	It Never Entered My Mind	Merc MG 20244, 824 864-1.
14426	Homework	Merc MG 20244.
14427	They Say It's Wonderful	Merc MG 20245, (E) 6199 035.
14428	The Touch Of Your Hand	Merc MG 20244.

90.   HAL MOONEY ORCHESTRA

NYC, Oct 31, 1956

14435	My Heart Stood Still	Merc MG 20245, 824 864-1.
14436	Let's Take An Old Fashioned Walk	Merc MG 20245, (E) 6199 035.
14437	My Ship	Merc MG 20245.
14438	A Tree In The Park	Merc MG 20244, 824 864-1, (E) 6199 035.
14439	A Ship Without A Sail	Merc MG 20244, 824 864-1, (E) 6199 035, Btm 10-5516.
14440	He's Only Wonderful	Merc MG 20245.

MG 20244 = SR 60041, MP2-100, (E)MPL 6522, (E)CMS 18019,
        (E)MMC 14024, Trip TLP 5589, (E) Memoir MOIR 127.
MG 20245 = SR 60078, MP2-100, (E)MPL 6523, (E)CMS 18023,
        (E)MMC 14026,
14413 - 14440 on Merc (J) 18PJ-1036.

91.   HAL MOONEY ORCHESTRA
                                         NYC, Nov 1, 1956

14445   But Not For Me   Merc MG 20244, Btm 10-5516.
14446   Poor Butterfly   Merc 71005, 30031, MG 20245,
                                   MG 20645, MG 60645, BM 687,
                                   (E)MEP 9519, (E)MPT 7528,
                                   (E)MT 151.
14447   Love Is A Random   Merc MG 20438, SR 60110.
               Thing
14448   If I Loved You   Wing MGW 12123, SRW 16123,
                                   (E)Wing WL 1083, Hlm HHP 8003,
                                   (E)WRC TP 230.
14449   September Song   Merc MG 20245, (E)MEP 9519.
14450   Lost In The Stars   Merc MG 20245, (E) 6619 035.

92.   HAL MOONEY ORCHESTRA
                                         NYC, Nov 2, 1956

14456   If This Isn't Love   Merc MG 20245, (E) 6619 035.
14457   It's Delovely   Wing MGW 12123,
                                   (E)Wing WL 1083, Hlm HHP 8003,
                                   (E)WRC TP 230.
14458   It's Love   Merc MG 20540, MG 60225.
14459   Lucky In Love   Merc MG 20244.
14460   It's Got To Be   Merc MG 20245, 824 864-1.
               Love
14461   Comes Love   Merc MG 20244.

MG 20244 = SR 60041, MP2-100, (E)MPL 6522, (E)CMS 18019,
           (E)MMC 14024, Trip TLP 5589, (E)Memoir Moir 127.
MG 20245 = SR 60078, MP2-100, (E)MPL 6523, (E)CMS 18023,
           (E)MMC 14026.

93.   HAL MOONEY ORCHESTRA
                                         NYC, Mid Nov, 1956

14473-12   The Bashful   Merc 71030, EP1-3507,
               Matador   Wing SRW 16123, (E)WRC TP 230.
14474-14   Leave It To Love   Merc 71030, EP1-3507, MG 20540
14475-5   Don't Let Me Love   Merc MG 20223, (E)MPT 6540.
               You
14476-5   The Second Time   Merc MG 20223, (E)MPT 6540.

94.   DAVID CARROLL ORCHESTRA
                                         NYC, Nov 29, 1956

14569   April Gave Me One   Merc 71085, Wing MGW 12123,
               More Day   SRW 16123, (E)WRC TP 230.
14570   I've Got A New   Merc 71020, EP1-3507,
               Heartache   Wing MGW 12123, SRW 16123,
                                   (E)WRC TP 230.
14571   Don't Look It Me   Merc MG 20438, SR 60110,
               That Way   (E)AMT 1087.
14572   The Banana Boat   Merc 71020, MG 20287, EP1-3507
               Song   (E)MT 139, (E)MEP 9511.

14445 - 14572 on Mer (J) 18PJ-1037.

95.   WITH HER TRIO
Jimmy Jones (p), Richard Davis (b), Roy Haynes (d).

NYC, Feb 14, 1957

14669-3	Words Can't Describe	EmArcy MG 36109.
14670-6	Pennies From Heaven	EmArcy MG 36109, (E)MPT 7518.
14671-4	All Of Me	EmArcy MG 36109.
14672-2	I Cried For You	EmArcy MG 36109.
14673-4	Linger Awhile	Merc (J).

MG 36109 = (E)EJL 1273, (E) 6336 713, Trip TLP 5551.

96.   HAL MOONEY ORCHESTRA
Including strings and Jimmy Jones (p).

NYC, March 20, 1957

15111	Someone To Watch Over Me	Merc MG 20310.
15112	A Foggy Day	Merc MG 20311.
15113	Bidin' My Time	Merc MG 20310, (E) 6619 035.
15114-3	He Loves And She Loves	Merc MG 20311, (E) 6619 035.
15115	Love Walked In	Merc MG 20311.
15116-5	Looking For A Boy	Merc MG 20311.
15117-2	I've Got A Crush On You	Merc MG 20310, (E)Vrv 2352 171
15118-1	Isn't It A Pity	Merc MG 20310, Btm 10-5516.
15119-3	Do It Again	Merc MG 20311, (E) 6619 035.
15120-7	How Long Has This Been Going On	Merc MG 20310, Btm 10-5516.
15121-4	Aren't You Kinda Glad We Did	Merc MG 20311.
15122	The Man I Love	Merc MG 20310, (E) 6619 035, Btm 10-5516.

14669 - 15122 on Merc (J) 18PJ 1038.

97.   HAL MOONEY ORCHESTRA

NYC, March 21, 1957

15123	Let's Call The Whole Thing Off	Merc MG 20311.
15124	They All Laughed	Merc MG 20311.
15125	Lorelei	Merc MG 20310, Btm 10-5516.
15126	I'll Build A Stairway To Paradise	Merc MG 20310, Btm 10-5516.

98.   HAL MOONEY ORCHESTRA

NYC, April 24, 1957

15313-11	Summertime	Merc MG 20310.
15314-6	Things Are Looking Up	Merc MG 20311.
15315-7	I Won't Say I Will	Merc MG 20311.
15316	Of Thee I Sing	Merc (J).
15316-7	Of Thee I Sing	Merc MG 20310, Btm 10-5516.
15317-5	My One And Only	Merc MG 20310.

MG 20310 = SR 60045, MP2-101, 814 187 1, (E)MPL 6526,
           (E)CMS 18011, (E)MMC 14095.
MG 20311 = SR 60045, MP2-101, 814 187 1, (E)MPL 6527,
           (E)CMS 18012, (E)MMC 14096.

99.   HAL MOONEY ORCHESTRA, DUET WITH BILLY ECKSTINE (Vcl)
                                    NYC, April 24, 1957

15318   Isn't It A Lovely   Merc MG 20316, MEP 27,
           Day   (E)MEP 9535, (E)ZEP 10121,
                              (E)SEZ 19023, (E)10027 MCE.
15319   Easter Parade   Merc MG 20316, (E)ZEP 10121,
                              (E)SEZ 19023.
15320   Now It Can Be Told Merc MG 20316, (E)MEP 9535.

15123 - 15320 on Merc (J) 18PJ-1039.

100. HAL MOONEY ORCHESTRA, DUET WITH BILLY ECKSTINE (vcl).
                                    NYC, April 25, 1957

15328   Alexander's Ragtime Merc 71393, MG 20316, MG 20813
           Band   MEP 27, (E)AMT 1020,
                              (E)MEP 9535, (E)ZEP 10002.
15329   I've Got My Love   Merc MG 20316, (E)MEP 9536,
           To Keep Me Warm   (E)ZEP 10108, (E)SEZ 19016.
15330   You're Just In   Merc MG 20316, MEP 27,
           Love   (E)MEP 9535, (E)ZEP 10108,
                              (E)SEZ 19016, (E)10027 MCE.
15331   My Man's Gone Now   Merc MG 20311.
           (SV solo)
15332   Cheek To Cheek   Merc MG 20316, (E)MEP 6536,
                              (E)ZEP 10108, (E)SEZ 19016,
                              (E) 6619 035.
15333   Remember   Merc MG 20316, MEP 27,
                              (E)MEP 9535, (E)ZEP 10108,
                              (E)SEP 19016, (E)10025 MCE.
15334   Always   Merc MG 20316, MG 20813,
                              (E)ZEP 10121, (E)SEZ 19023,
                              (E)10025 MCE.

MG 20316 = SR 60002, (E)MPL 6530, (E)CMS 18002, (E)MMC 14035,
           (E)SMCL 20155, (E)SMWL 21017, (E) 6463 041,
           (E) 6641 868, (E)Phi Sonic 037.

101. HAL MOONEY ORCHESTRA, DUET WITH BILLY ECKSTINE (vcl).
                                    NYC, April 26, 1957

15336   Passing Strangers   Merc 71122, (E)MT 164,
                              (E)AMT 1071, (E)ZEP 10022,
                              (E)10025 MCE, (E)MCL 20155,
                              (E) 6619 035, (E) 6300 039,
                              (E) 6641 868, (E) 6612 055,
                              (E)Phi Sonic 031,
                              (E)CBS 6612 040,
                              (E)Vrv 819 442-1.
15339   The Door Is Open   Merc 71122, (E)MT 164,
                              (E)MPT 7525, (E)ZEP 10022,
                              (E)10015 MCE.

102.   HAL MOONEY ORCHESTRA

NYC, Circa May, 1957

15356   Linger Awhile   unissued

103.   HAL MOONEY ORCHESTRA

NYC, June 3, 1957

15467-4	You'll Find Me	Merc MG 20540,
	There	Wing MGW 12123, SRW 16123,
		(E)WRC TP 230.
15468-1	Please Mr. Brown	Merc (J).
15468-9	Please Mr. Brown	Merc 71157, MG 20540,
		(E)MT 176, (E)MEP 9525.
15469-7	Band Of Angels	Merc 71157,(E)MT 176.
15470-6	Slow Down	Merc MG 20617, SR 60617,
		(E)20042 SMCL.

104.   HAL MOONEY ORCHESTRA, DUET WITH BILLY ECKSTINE (vcl)

NYC, July 12, 1957

15473-17	Goodnight Kiss	Merc (J).
15474-13	No Limit	Merc 71393, (E)AMT 1020,
		(E)ZEP 10002.

15328 - 15474 on Merc (J) 18PJ-1040.

105.   WITH HER TRIO
Jimmy Jones (p), Richard Davis (b), Roy Haynes (d).

Mr Kelly's, Chicago, Aug 6, 1957

15739	September In The	Merc MG 20326, 2EM 412.
	Rain	
15470	Willow Weep For Me	Merc MG 20326.
15471	Just One Of Those	Merc MG 20326, 2EM 412.
	Things	
15472	Be Anything, But	Merc MG 20326, 2EM 412.
	Darling Be Mine	
15743	Thou Swell	Merc MG 20326, 2EM 412,
		824 864-1, (E)Phi Sonic 031.
15744	Stairway To The	Merc MG 20326, 2EM 412.
	Stars	
15745	Honeysuckle Rose	Merc MG 20326.
15746	Just A Gigolo	Merc MG 20326.
15747	How High The Moon	Merc MG 20326, 2EM 412.
15748	Dream	Merc (J).
15479	I'm Gonna Sit	Merc (J).
	Right Down And	
	Write Myself A	
	Letter	
15480	It's Got To Be	Merc (J).
	Love	

MG 20326 = (E)MPL 6542, (E)MVL 303.

106. WITH HER TRIO
Personnel as Aug 6, 1957.

Chicago, Aug 7, 1957

| 15752 | Alone | Merc (J). |
| 15753 | It's Got To Be Love | Merc (J). |

15739 - 15753 on Merc (J) 18PJ-1041.

107. WITH HER TRIO
Personnel as Aug 6, 1957.

Chicago, Aug 8,1957

15756	If This Isn't Love	Merc (J).
15757	Embraceable You	Merc (J).
15758	Lucky In Love	Merc (J).
15759	Dancing In The Dark	Merc (J).
15760	Poor Butterfly	Merc (J).
15761	Sometimes I'm Happy	Merc (J).
15762	I Cover The Waterfront	Merc (J).

108. HAL MOONEY ORCHESTRA

NYC, Oct 29, 1957

15988-12	Sweet Affection	Merc MG 20438, SR 60110, Wing MGW 12280, (E)AMT 1087.
15589-8	Meet Me Halfway	Wing MGW 12123.
15990-6	What's So Bad About It	Merc 71326, MG 20438, SR 60110 Wing MGW 12280, (E)AMT 1222, (E)MT 222.

109. HAL MOONEY ORCHESTRA

NYC, Nov 26, 1957

16143-7	That Old Black Magic	Merc (J).
16143-8	That Old Black Magic	Merc MG 20438, Wing MGW 12280.
16144-11	I've Got The World On A String	Merc (J).
16144-13	I've Got The World On A String	Merc MG 20438, Wing MGW 12280, Hlm HHP 8003.
16145-4	Hit The Road To Dreamland	Wing MGW 12123.

15756 - 16145 On Merc (J) 18PJ-1042.

110. HAL MOONEY ORCHESTRA

NYC, Nov 11, 1957

| 16205-6 | Gone Again | Merc 71235, MG 20540, SR 60225 |
| 16206-9 | The Next Time Around | Merc MG 20540, SR 60225. |

111.   RAY ELLIS ORCHESTRA

NYC,Circa Nov/Dec, 1957

16593   Careless   Merc 71433, MG 20438, SR 60110
                                    Wing MGW 12280, (E)AMT 1044.

112.   HAL MOONEY ORCHESTRA

NYC, Dec 18, 1957

16927-11   Friendly Enemies   Merc MG 20438, SR 60110,
                                    Wing MGW 12280.
16928-8   Are You Certain   Merc 71407, MG 20438, SR 60110
                                    Wing MGW 12280, (E)ZEP 10011,
                                    (E)AMT 1029.

113.   MEMBERS OF THE COUNT BASIE BAND
Thad Jones (cond, tp), Wendell Culley (cond), Snooky Young,
Joe Newman (tp), Henry Coker, Al Grey, Benny Powell (tb),
Marshall Royal (as, cl), Frank Wess (as, ts, fl), Frank
Foster, Billy Mitchell (ts), Charlie Fowkles (bar), Ronnell
Bright (p), Freddie Green (g), Richard Davis (b), Sonny
Payne (d).

NYC, Jan 5, 1958

16931-1   Stardust   Merc SNP-133.
16931-2   Stardust   Merc SNP-133.
16931-3   Stardust (part)   Merc SNP-133.
16931-4   Stardust (edited)   Merc SNP-133, MG 20441,
                                    (E)ZEP 10101, Btm 10-551.
16932-7   Doodlin'   Merc (J).
16932-12   Doodlin'   Merc 71642, MG 20441.
16933-9   Darn That Dream   Merc (J).
16933-10   Darn That Dream   Merc (J).
16933-11   Darn That Dream   Merc MG 20441, (E)ZEP 10115,
                                    Btm 10-551.

16933 accompanied by tp, ts, p, g, b, and d only.
MG 20441 = SR 60116, (E)MMC 14021, (E)CMS 18058, (E)FJL 129,
          and Trip TLP 5562.

114.   RAY ELLIS ORCHESTRA

NYC, Jan 7, 1958

17010-8   Mary Contrary   Merc 71742, MG 20438, SR 60110
                                    Wing MGW 12280.
17041-7   Separate Ways   Merc 71443, MG 20438, SR 60110
                                    Wing MGW 12280, (E)AMT 1044.
17052   Broken-Hearted   Merc 71477, 30092, MG 20438,
            Melody   MG 20511, MG 20645, SR 60110,
                                    SR 60645, BM 687, (E)AMT 1057,
                                    (E)MEP 10041, (E)ZEP 10041,
                                    (E)EP1-3396, Hlm HHP 8003.

MG 20438 = SR 60438.

115. WITH HER TRIO PLUS 4 GUESTS
Ronnell Bright (p), Richard Davis (b), Roy Haynes (d).
Guests :- Thad Jones, Wendell Culley (tp), Henry Coker (tb),
Frank Wess (ts).
                        Live, London House, Chicago, March 7, 1958

17505	Detour Ahead	Merc MG 20383.
17506	Three Little Words	Merc MG 20383, 2EM 412, (E)ZEP 10030.
17507	Speak Low	Merc MG 20383, 2EM 412.
17508	Like Someone In Love	Merc MG 20383, 2EM 412, (E)ZEP 10030.
17509	My Buddy	rejected.
17510	You'd Be So Nice To Come Home To	Merc MG 20383.
17511	I'll String Along With You	Merc MG 20383, 2EM 412, (E)ZEP 10030.
17512	All Of You	Merc MG 20383, 2EM 412.
17513	Thanks For The Memory	Merc MG 20383, 2EM 412.

MG 20383 = SR 60020, (E)MMC 14001 and Trip TLP 5595
Note;-17508 includes the opening announcement and is probably
    the first recorded track in this live performance.

116. HAL MOONEY ORCHESTRA AND CHORUS
                                    NYC, March 29, 1958

17079-8	Too Much,Too Soon	Merc 71326, (E)MT 212.
17080-10	Padre	Merc 71303, MG 20540, SR 60225 (E)MT 212.
17081-6	Spin Little Bottle	Merc 71303, (E)MT 212.

16205 - 17052 and 17079 - 17081 on Merc (J) 18PJ 1043
                    except 16931 -1 to -3

117. QUINCY JONES ORCHESTRA
Zoot Sims, Jo Hrasko, William Boucaya, Marcel Hrasko (saxes),
Michel Hausser (vib), Ronnell Bright (p), Pierre Cullaz (g),
Richard Davis (b-1), Pierre Michelot (b-2), Kenny Clarke (d),
unknown strings, Quincy Jones (arr).
                                    Paris, July 7, 1958

17781	Please Be Kind (1)	Merc EP1-4042, MG 20370, SR-627.
17782	The Midnight Sun Will Never Set (1)	Merc MG 20370, SR-627, (E)ZEP 10087, CTN 18029.
17783	Live For Love (1)	Merc MG 20370, (E)ZEP 10087.
17784	Misty (1)	Merc 71477, 30093, MG 20370, MG 20511, MG 20645, SR 60645, EP1-4042, (E)AMT 1037, (E)ZEP 10041, (E)SMWL 21018, (E) 6619 035, BM 638, Hml HHP 8003.
17785	I'm Lost (2)	Merc 20370, SR-627.
17786	Love Me (2)	Merc MG 20370,(E)ZEP 10087.
17787	That's All (2)	Merc MG 20370, (E)ZEP 10087, Hlm HHP 8003.

118.   QUINCY JONES ORCHESTRA
Maurice Vander, Ronnell Bright (p), Richard Davis (b), Roger
Paraboschi or Kansas Fields (d), 35 violins, 8 cellos and
violas, 7 woodwinds, Quincy Jones (arr, cond).
                                          Paris, July 12, 1958

17788	Day By Day	Merc EP1-4042, MG 20370, SR-627, Hml HHP 8003.
17789	Gone With The Wind	Merc EP1-4042, MG 20370, (E)ZEP 10041, (E)MEP 14231.
17790	I'll Close My Eyes	Merc MG 20370, (E)ZEP 10087.
17791	The Thrill Is Gone	Merc MG 20370.

MG 20370 = SR 60038, (E)MMC 14011, (E)CMS 18003, (E)MPT 7518,
          Wing MGW 12360, SRW 16360, (E) Memoir MOIR 113.

119.   HAL MOONEY ORCHESTRA
                                          NYC, Sept 26,1958

17990-7	Cool Baby	Merc 71407, (E)AMT 1029, (E)ZEP 10011, Wing MGW 12237, (E)Wing WL 1083.
18018-10	Everything I Do	Merc 71380, (E)AMT 1010, (E)ZEP 10011.
18019-14	I Ain't Hurtin'	Merc 71380, (E)AMT 1010, (E)ZEP 10011.
18020-6	Disillusioned Heart	Merc (J).

17781 - 18020 on Merc (J) 18PJ-1045.

120.   MEMBERS OF THE COUNT BASIE ORCHESTRA
Personnel as Jan 5, 1958
                                          NYC, Dec 15, 1958
| 17413-17 | Smoke Gets In Your Eyes | Merc MG 20441, Btm 10-5516. |

121.   MEMBERS OF THE COUNT BASIE ORCHESTRA
Personnel as Jan 5, 1958.
                                          NYC, Dec 23, 1958

17423-14	Moonlight in Vermont	Merc MG 20441, MG 20645, (E)ZEP 10101.
17424-16	Cheek To Cheek	Merc MG 20441.
17425-16	Missing You	Merc MG 20441, (E)ZEP 10115.
17426-3	Just One Of Those Things	Merc MG 20441, (E)ZEP 10101, (E) 6619 035, Btm 10-5516.
17427-3	No Count Blues	Merc MG 20441, (E)ZEP 10115.

MG 20441 = SR 60116, (E)MMC 14021, (E)CMS 18058, (E)FJL 129,
          Trip TLP 5562.
17413 - 17427 on Merc (J) 18PJ-1044.

122.   BELFORD C. HENDRICKS ORCHESTRA
                                          NYC, Sept 2, 1959

| 19016-2 | I Should Care | Merc MG 20580. |
| 19017-3 | For All We Know | Merc 71669, Wing MGW 12237, (E)Wing WL 1083, Hlm HHP 8003. |

```
19018-4    My Ideal               Merc MG 20617.
19019-5    You're My Baby         Merc 71562, MG 20581, EP1-3396
19020-5    Smooth Operator        Merc 71519, MG 20493,
                                  MG 20645, SR 60172, SR 60645,
                                  EP1-3396, (E)AMT 1071,
                                  (E)ZEP 10054, Bir BM 687.
10921-8    Maybe It's Because     Merc 71519, MG 20617,
                                  (E) 20042 SMCL, (E)ZEP 10054.
19022-2    Our Waltz              Merc 71610, MG 20617,
                                  (E) 20042 SMCL.
19023-2    Never In A Million     Merc MG 20617.
              Years
19024-1    Close To You           Merc 71702, MG 20580,
                                  (E)SMWL 21054, Bir BM 687.
19025-2    Eternally              Merc 71562, EP1-3396, MG 20645
                                  MG 20617, SR 60645,
                                  (E)AMT 1080, (E) 20042 SMCL,
                                  Bir BM 687.
```

19016 - 19017 on Merc (J) 18PJ-1045.

123. BELFORD C. HENDRICKS ORCHESTRA

NYC, Late 1959

```
19382      Some Other Spring      Merc 71610, MG 20617,
                                  (E) 20042 SMCL.
```

124. FRED NORMAN ORCHESTRA

NYC, Late 1959

```
19626      Say It Isn't So        Merc Merc MG 20580.
19627      If You Are But A       Merc 71742, MG 20580.
              Dream
19628      Maybe You'll Be        Merc 71624, MG 20580.
              There
19629      (All Of A Sudden)      Merc MG 20617.
              My Heart Sings
19630      There's No You         Merc MG 20580.
19631      Missing You            Merc MG 20580.
19632      Please                 Merc MG 20580.
19633      Funny                  Merc MG 20580.
19634      I've Got To Talk       Merc MG 20580.
              To My Heart
19635      Out Of This World      Merc 71702, MG 20580.
19636      Last Night When We     Merc MG 20580.
              Were Young
19637      Through A Long And     Merc MG 20617.
              Sleepless Night
```

125. BELFORD C. HENDRICKS ORCHESTRA

NYC, Late 1959

```
19638      I'll Never Be The      Merc MG 20580.
              Same
19639      Through The Years      Merc 71699, MG 20617,
```

MG 20580 = SR 60240, (E)MMC 14059, (E)CSM 18040.
MG 20617 = SR 60617, (E) 20042 SMCL.
19018 - 19639 on Merc (J) 18PJ-1046.

126. CLARK TERRY QUARTET
Clark Terry (tp, vcl), Ronnell Bright (p), Richard Davis (b),
Roy Haynes (d).

Europe Circa 1960

| | Scat Blues | (I) Euro Jazz EJ 1019.
(I)I Giganti Del Jazz 22. |

127. JIMMY JONES ORCHESTRA
Harry Edison (tp), Gerald Sanfino (fl, ts), Janet Soyer
(harp), unknown strings, Ronnell Bright (p), Barry Galbraith
(g), Richard Davis or George Duvivier (b), Percy Brice (d).

NYC, 19 April, 1960

14950	My Ideal	Roul R(S) 52046, RE 103, (E)RE 103, Accord SN 7195.
14951	Hands Across The Table	Roul R(S) 52046, FCS 9085, WMGS-2, Accord SN 7195.
14952	You've Changed	Roul R(S) 52046, R(S) 52050, RE 107, F-9004, Accord SN 7195
14953	Crazy He Calls Me	Roul R(S) 52046, R(S) 52057, FCS 9085, (E)Eros 9098.
14954	I'll Be Seeing You	Roul R(S) 52046, RE 103, FCS 9085, (E)RE 103, (E) Rou 1022, (E)EMB 3375.
14955	Stormy Weather	Roul R(S) 52046, R(S) 52057, (E)EMB 3375.
14956	The More I See You	Roul REP 1003, R(S) 52046, (E)EMB 3375, (E)Eros 8098.
14957	Star Eyes	Roul REP 1003, R(S) 52046.
14958	Trees	Roul R(S) 52046, R(S) 52050, WGMS-2.
14959	Moon Over Miami	Roul REP 1003, R(S) 52046, R(S) 52053, F 5067, FCS 9058.
14960	Dreamy	Roul R(S) 52046.
14961	Why Was I Born	Roul R(S) 52046, R(S) 52050, F 9004, WGMS-2.

R(S) 52046 = Forum F 9034, (E)Col 33SX 1252, SCX 3324,
            (E)WRC 440. also Emus ES 12007 except 14952,
            14954 and 14959.

128. JOE REISMAN ORCHESTRA
Bob Alexander, Bob Byrnes, Dick Hixon (tb), Stan Webb
(as, fl), unknown strings, Ronnell Bright (p, or celeste*),
John Pizzarelli, Al Chernet, Art Ryerson (g), Ted Sommers
(d), unknown perc, vibes and bells etc.,
plus organ and male chorus **.

NYC, May 5, 1960

15006	Serenata	Roul 4285, REP 1026, R(S) 52108, R(S) 52062, GG-67, (E) Rou 1022, (E)Col DB 4542, (E)SCX 1645, Emus ES 12015.
15007	My Dear Little Sweetheart*	Roul 4256, R(S) 52109, (E) Rou 1022, (E)Col DB 4491.
15008	Let's**	Roul 4285, REP 1026, (E)Col DB 4542.

15009   Ooh,What A Day   Roul 4256, REP 1003,
                                       (E)Col DB 4491.

129. JEFF ALEXANDER ORCHESTRA
                                                       circa 1960

               The Awakening   Canadian American CALP 1003.
               Fan My Brow   Canadian American CALP 1003.

130. WITH HER TRIO
Ronnell Bright (p), Richard Davis (b), Percy Bryce (d).
          Madison Square Garden Jazz Festival, NYC, June 2, 1960

               What Is This Thing   VJC-1015-2 (CD).
                 Called Love
               Gone With The Wind   VJC-1015-2 (CD).
               All Of Me   VJC-1015-2 (CD).
               Don't Blame Me   VJC-1015-2 (CD).
               Just One Of Those   VJC-1015-2 (CD).
                 Things
               Misty   JVC-1015-2 (CD).
               Sometimes I'm   JVC-1015-2 (CD).
                 Happy

131. COUNT BASIE ORCHESTRA, DUET WITH JOE WILLIAMS (vcl)
Sonny Cohn, Thad Jones, Joe Newman, Snooky Young (tp), Henry
Coker, Al Grey, Benny Powell (tb), Marshall Royal, Frank
Wess, Frank Foster, Billy Mitchell, Charlie Fowlkes (reeds),
Freddie Green (g), Count Basie (p, cond), Eddie Jones (b),
Sonny Payne (d).
          Madison Square Garden Jazz Festival, NYC, June 2, 1960

               Teach Me Tonight   VJC-1015-2 (CD).

132. COUNT BASIE ORCHESTRA, DUET WITH JOE WILLIAMS (vcl)
Sonny Cohn, Thad Jones, Lennie Johnson, Snooky Young (tp),
Henry Coker, Quentin Jackson, Benny Powell (tb), Marshall
Royal (as, ts, fl), Frank Wess, Budd Johnson (ts), Charlie
Fowlkes (bar), Count Basie (p), Freddie Green (g), Eddie
Jones (b), Sonny Payne (d).
                                       NYC, July 19, 1960

15285   Until I Met You   unissued
                 (SV solo)
15286   If I Were A Bell   Roul 4273, REP 1008, RL 21104,
                                       (E)Col DB 5411.
15287   Teach Me Tonight   Roul 4273, REP 1008, RL 21104,
                                       WGMS-2, (E)Col DB 5411.

133. BILLY MAY ORCHESTRA
unknown tps, tbs, reeds, g, p, b, d, perc and vocal chorus.
                         United Recorders, LA, Oct 8, 1960

15493   Green Leaves Of   Roul 4343, (E)Rou 1022.
                 Summer
15494   Them There Eyes   Roul 4343, (E)Rou 1022.
15495   Don't Go To   Roul (E)Rou 1022.
                 Strangers
15496   Love   Roul (E)Rou 1022.

134. JIMMY JONES ORCHESTRA
Harry Edison (tp), unknown tb, ts, bar, Jimmy Jones (p, ldr),
g, b, and d.
                              Capitol Studio, NYC, Oct 11, 1960

15468	Jump For Joy	rejected.
15469	You Stepped Out Of A Dream	rejected.
15470	Wrap Your Troubles In Dreams	rejected.

135. JIMMY JONES ORCHESTRA
Harry Edison (tp), 3 unknown woodwinds, Jimmy Jones
(p, cond), unknown g, b and d.
                              Capitol Studio, NYC, Oct 12, 1960

15472	What Do You See In Her	Roul R(S) 52060.
15473	Trouble Is A Man	Roul R(S) 52060.
15474	I'm Gonna Laugh You Right Out Of My Life	Roul RJB 6, R(S) 52060.
15475	Every Time I See You	Roul R(S) 52060.

136. JIMMY JONES ORCHESTRA
as Oct 11, 1960.
                              Capitol Studio, NYC, Oct 13, 1960

15476	When Your Lover Has Gone	Roul REP 1026, R(S) 52060, (E)RE 103, (E) 2682 032, Accord SN 7159.
15477	Ain't No Use	Roul REP 1028, R(S) 52060, SR33-8044, (E)RE 103, (E) 2682 032, WGMS-2, Smi P-11895.
15478	Gloomy Sunday	Roul R(S) 52060, (E)RE 103, (E) 2682 032.
15479	Somebody Else's Dream	Roul R(S) 52060.

137. JIMMY JONES ORCHESTRA
as Oct 11, 1960.
                              Capitol Studio, NYC, Oct 19, 1960

15468	Jump For Joy	Roul REP 1028, R(S) 52060, R(S) 52109, (E)Rou 1020, (E) 26082 032.
15469	You Stepped Out Of A Dream	Roul REP 1028, R(S) 52060, (E)Rou 1020, (E) 2682 032, WGMS-2, Accord SN 7195.
15470	Wrap Your Troubles In Dreams	Roul RJB 6, REP 1026, R(S) 25060, (E) 2682 032.
15516	Have You Met Miss Jones	Roul REP 1028, R(S) 52060, R(S) 52075, SR33-8044, (E)Rou 1020, (E) 2682 032, Accord SN 7195.

R(S) 25060 = Emus ES 12009, (E)Col 33SX 1340, (E)Col SCX 3390
         (E)MFP 1107, (E)Saga 8144.

138. JOE REISMAN ORCHESTRA
unknown strings, reeds, vibes, g, p, b, d. *omit strings and
vibes.

NYC, Jan 5, 1961

15776	What's The Use	Roul 4325, (E)Rou 1022, (E)Col 45DB 4634.
15777	Wallflower Waltz	Roul 4547, R(S) 52109, RE 105, (E)Rou 1022.
15778	True Believer*	Roul 4325, (E)Rou 1022, (E)Col 45DB 4634.

139. JOE REISMAN ORCHESTRA
as Jan 5, 1961 omit vibes add perc/bells.
*omit strings and reeds, add organ and bass guitar.
** alto sax solo by Joe Leriza.

NYC, Jan 9, 1961

15797	April**	Roul 4359, (E)Rou 1022.
15798	If Not For You	Roul (E)Rou 1022.
15799	Oh, Lover*	Roul 4359, (E)Rou 1022.

140. COUNT BASIE ORCHESTRA
as July 14,1960, omit duet with Joe Williams (vcl).

NYC, Jan 10, 1961

15726	You Go To My Head	Roul R(S) 52061, RE 107, 9045-107, (E)Pye GH 869, GT-15
15727	You Turned The Tables On Me	Roul R(S) 52061, WMGS-2, WPOM-6, (E)Pye GH 869.

141. COUNT BASIE ORCHESTRA
as Jan 10, 1961.

NYC, Jan 11, 1961

15728	The Gentleman Is A Dope	Roul R(S) 52061, RE 107, 9045-107, (E)Pye GH 869.

142. COUNT BASIE ORCHESTRA
as Jan 10, 1961.

NYC, Jan 12, 1961

15729	Mean To Me	Roul R(S) 52061, R(S) 52111, RE 107, 9045-107, (E)Rou 1020, (E)Pye GH 869.
15730	Lover Man	Roul R(S) 52061, RE 107, 9045-107, (E)Rou 1020, (E)Pye GH 869.
15731	Alone	Rou R(S) 52061.

143. COUNT BASIE ORCHESTRA
as Jan 10, 1961. omit Jackson, Lennie and Budd Johnson, add
Joe Newman (tp), Al Grey (tb), Billy Mitchell (ts).

* NYC, Jan 13, 1961

15791	I Cried For You	Roul R(S) 52061, (E)Rou 1020.

15792	Little Man You've Had A Busy Day	Roul R(S) 52061, R(S) 52075, RE 103.
15793	Until I Met You	Roul R(S) 52061, R(S) 52111.
15794	There Are Such Things	Roul R(S) 52061.
15795	Perdido	Roul R(S) 52061, Forum F 9056, (E)RE 103, (E)Rou 1020, (E)Pye GH 869.

* Chris Sheridan (Basie Bio/Discographer) gives this date as
  March 9, 1961, listed date is from Roulette archives.
R (S) 52061 = (E) 2682 031 (except 15726, 731, and 792),
          Emus ES 12010, (E)Col 33SX 1360,
          (E)Col SCX 3403, (E)Allegro All 812 (except
          15794), (E)Eros 8074 (except 15795),
          Book of the Month Club 10-5516.

144. MARTY MANNING ORCHESTRA
unknown strings, saxes, g, p, b, and d.
* omit saxes, add electric mandolin, marimba and percussion.
                                        NYC, June, 1961

16116	Untouchable	Roul 4378.
16117	Sleepy	unissued
16118	The Hills Of Assisi	Roul 4378

145. MUNDELL LOWE (g) and GEORGE DUVIVIER (b).
                                  NYC, Early July, 1961

	Just Squeeze Me	rejected
	Body And Soul	rejected
	Through The Years	uniss:ed

146. MUNDELL LOWE (g) and GEORGE DUVIVIER (b).
                                  NYC, July 18, 1961

16157	Wonder Why	Roul R(S) 52070.
16158	My Favorite Things	Roul RJB-5, R(S) 52070, R(S) 52109, (E)EMB 3375.
16159	Great Day	Roul 4397, R(S) 52070, (E)Rou 1020.
16160	Sophisticated Lady	Roul R(S) 52070, (E)EMB 3375.
16161	Ev'ry Time We Say Goodbye	Roul R(S) 52070, (E)Rou 1020, WGMS-2.
16162	Ill Wind	Roul RJB-5, R(S) 52070.
16163	In A Sentimental Mood	Roul R(S) 52070, WGMS-2, (E)EMB 3375.
16164	If Love Is Good To Me	Roul 4397, R(S) 52070, WGMS-2.
16165	Easy To Love	Roul R(S) 52070.
16166	Vanity	Roul R(S) 52070.

R(S) 52070 = (E) 2682 032, Emus ES 12025, (E)Col 33SX 1405,
          (E)MFP 1130.

147. QUINCY JONES ORCHESTRA

NYC, Early Feb, 1962

16495	The Best Is Yet To Come	Roul R(S) 52082, (E)RE 103.
16496	Baubles,Bangles And Beads	unissued
16497	So Long	Roul R(S) 52082, (E) 2682 043. (E)RE 103, (E)Bravo EP 381.
16498	I Could Write A Book	Roul 4443, R(S) 52082, (E) 2682 043, (E)Col 45DB 4901
16499	Moonglow	Roul R(S) 52082, (E) 2682 043, (E)RE 103, (E)Col 45DB 4901, (E)Bravo EP 381.
16500	Witchcraft	Roul R(S) 52082, (E) 2682 043, MGMS-2.
16501	On Green Dolphin Street	Roul R(S) 52082, (E) 2682 043.
16502	Maria	Roul R(S) 52082, R(S) 52109, (E)Rou 1021, WGMS-2, (E)EMB SE 8000, (E)Eros 8098, (E)Bravo EP 381.
16503	The Second Time Around	Roul R(S) 52082, (E)RE 103,
16504	Invitation	Roul R(S) 52082.
16505	You're Mine You	Roul R(S) 52082, (E)RE 103.
16506	Fly Me To The Moon	Roul 4443, R(S) 52082, R(S) 52109, MGMS-2, Emus ES 12015, (E)Col 33SX 1645, (E)Eros 8099

R(S) 52082 = R 42019, (E)Col 33SX 1438, (E)Col SCX 3444,
         (E)Allegro All 801.

148. QUINCY JONES ORCHESTRA

NYC, March, 1962

16543	Baubles, Bangles And Beads	Roul R(S) 52087, (E) 2682 043.
16544	One Mint Julep	Roul 4413, (E)Rou 1022, (E)Col 45DB 4807.
16545	Mama, He Treats Your Daughter Mean	Roul 4413, R(S) 52109, (E)RE 103, (E)Rou 1022, (E)Col 45DB 4807.
16546	The Best Is Yet To Come	unissued

149. WITH HER TRIO WITH SPECIAL GUEST WOODY HERMAN (cl).
probably Ronnell Bright (p), Richard Davis (b), Percy
Bryce (d).

NYC, Circa 1961/62

Day In,Day Out	VJC-1015-2 (CD).
But Not For Me	VJC-1015-2 (CD).
The More I See You	VJC-1015-2 (CD).
On Green Dolphin Street	VJC-1015-2 (CD).
Just One Of Those Things	VJC-1015-2 (CD).

	I'll Be Seeing You	VJC-1015-2 (CD).
	I Cried For You	VJC-1015-2 (CD).
	Poor Butterfly	VJC-1015-2 (CD).

150. DON COSTA ORCHESTRA

NYC, July 23/25, 1962

16871	I Remember You	Roul R(S) 52091, SEPR-1-328, (E)RE 103, (E)Rou 1021.
16872	I Fall In Love Too Easily	Roul R(S) 52091, (E)Rou 1021.
16873	I Hadn't Anyone 'Till You	Roul R(S) 52091.
16874	Glad To Be Unhappy	Roul R(S) 52091, (E)Rou 1021.
16877	Oh, You Crazy Moon	Roul R(S) 52091, SERP-1-328.
16878	Snowbound	Roul 4497, R(S) 52091, SERP-1-328.
16879	Look To Your Heart	Roul R(S) 52091.

151. DON COSTA ORCHESTRA

NYC, July 27, 1962

16903	Stella By Starlight	Roul R(S) 52091, R(S) 52109, (E)RE 103.
16904	Blah, Blah, Blah	Roul R(S) 52091.
16905	What's Good About Goodbye	Roul R(S) 52091.
16906	Spring Can Really Hang You Up The Most	Roul R(S) 52091, (E)Rou 1021.

R(S) 52091 = (E)Col 33SX 1542, (E)Col SCX 3489.

152. BARNEY KESSEL (g) and JOE COMFORT (b).

LA, Aug 7, 1962

16913	I Understand	Roul R(S) 52118.
16914	Key Largo	Roul R(S) 52118, New World NW 295.
16915	The Very Thought Of You	Roul R(S) 52118.
16916	Just Squeeze Me	Roul R(S) 52118.
16917	When Sunny Gets Blue	Roul R(S) 52118, RE 103, (E)RE 103.
16918	Baby, Won't You Please Come Home	Roul R(S) 52118.
16919	When Lights Are Low	Roul R(S) 53118, (E)Rou 1021.
16920	All I Do Is Dream Of You	Roul R(S) 52118.
16921	Just In Time	Roul R(S) 52118, (E)Rou 1020.
16922	All Or Nothing At All	Roul R(S) 52118, (E)Rou 1021.
16923	Goodnight Sweetheart	Roul R(S) 52118.
16924	unknown title	unissued

R(S) 52118 = (E) 2682 032.

153. BENNY CARTER ORCHESTRA
possibly including Frank Foster (ts), Joe Comfort (b) and
other members of the Basie Orchestra.
                              United Recorders LA, Aug 8, 1962

16925	Nobody Else But Me	Roul R(S) 52092, RE 105.
16926	Falling In Love With Love	Roul R(S) 52092.
16927	I Believe In You	Roul 5416, R(S) 52092.
16928	A Garden In The Rain	Roul R(S) 52092, (E)Col 45DB 7378.
16929	I'm Gonna Live 'Till I Die	Roul R(S) 52092.
16930	I Can't Give You Anything But Love	Roul R(S) 52092, R(S) 52108, (E)Rou 1020, Emus ES 12015, (E)Col 45DB 7378, (E)Col 33SX 1645.
16931	After You've Gone	Roul R(S) 52092.
16932	Moonlight On The Ganges	Roul R(S) 52092, R(S) 52109.
16933	The Lady's In Love With You	Roul R(S) 52092, RE 105, (E)RE 103.
16934	The Trolley Song	Roul R(S) 52092.
16935	Honeysuckle Rose	Roul R(S) 52092, (E)Rou 1020.
16936	Great Day	Roul R(S) 52092.

R(S) 52092 = (E)Col 33SX 1523, (E)Col SCX 3479, (E) 2682 032.

154. MARTY MANNING ORCHESTRA
unknown strings, woodwinds, frhs, g, p, b, and d.
                              NYC, Feb 13, 1963

17251	There'll Be Other Times	Roul 4482, R(S) 52100.
17252	Don't Go To Strangers	Roul R(S) 52100.
17253	Enchanted Wall	unissued
17254	Call Me Irresponsible	Roul 4482, R(S) 52100, R(S) 52109, (E)RE 103.

155. MARTY MANNING ORCHESTRA
                              NYC, Feb 27 , 1963

17255	Star Eyes	Roul R(S) 52100.
17256	Do You Remember	Roul R(S) 52100.
17257	I'll Never Be The Same	Roul R(S) 52100.
17258	I Was Telling Him About You	Roul R(S) 52100, RE 105.

156. MARTY MANNING ORCHESTRA
                              NYC, March 5 and 8, 1963

17265	Icy Stone	Roul R(S) 52100, (E)RE 103.
17266	As Long As He Needs Me	Roul R(S) 52100, (E)RE 103, (E)EMB 3375, (E)Eros 8098.
17267	One Upon A Summertime	Roul 4497, R(S) 52100.
17268	Bewildered	Roul R(S) 52100.

17277   Within Me I Know   Roul R(S) 52100.

R(S) 52100 = (E)Col 33SX 1592, (E)Col SCX 3507.

157.   MARTY MANNING ORCHESTRA
                                            NYC, March 11, 1963

17280   Full Moon And   Roul R(S) 52123.
               Empty Arms
17281   Ah, Sweet Mystery   Roul R(S) 52123.
               Of Life
17282   Because   Roul R(S) 52123.
17283   Be My Love   Roul R(S) 52123.
17284   Intermezzo   Roul R(S) 52123.
17285   My Reverie   Roul R(S) 52123.
17286   Moonlight Love   Roul R(S) 52123.
17287   I Give To You   Roul R(S) 52123.

158.   GERALD WILSON ORCHESTRA
unknown tp, ts, g, p, b and d.   *omit tp and ts.
                            United Recorders LA, May 29, 1963

17528   I Guess I'll Hang   Roul R(S) 52116.
               My Tears Out To
               Dry
17529   'Round Midnight   Roul R(S) 52116, (E)Rou 1021,
                                   (E) 2682 043.
17530   Midnight Sun   Roul R(S) 52116, (E)RE 103,
                                   (E) 2682 043.
17531   Easy Street   Roul R(S) 52116, (E) 2682 043.
17532   In Love In Vain*   Roul R(S) 52116.

159.   GERALD WILSON ORCHESTRA
                            United Recorders LA, May 31, 1963

17533   A Taste Of Honey   Roul 4604, R(S) 52116,
                                   (E) 2682 043.
17534   Moanin'   Roul R(S) 52116, (E) 2682 043.

160.   GERALD WILSON ORCHESTRA
                            United Recorders LA, June 6, 1963

17535   What Kind Of Fool   Roul R(S) 52116, (E)EMB 3375,
               Am I   (E)Eros 8098.
17536   The Good Life*   Roul R(S) 52116, (E) 2682 043.

161.   GERALD WILSON ORCHESTRA
                            United Recorders LA, June 12, 1963

17537   Sermonette   Roul R(S) 52116, (E) 2682 043.
17538   The Gravy Waltz   Roul R(S) 52116.
17539   Baby, Won't You   Roul R(S) 52116, (E) 2682 043.
               Please Come Home

R(S) 52116 = (E)Col 33SX 1726, (E)Col SCX 3553.

162.   BENNY CARTER ORCHESTRA
Gerald Wilson (tp), unknown woodwinds and rhythm
                                    LA, June 13-16, 1963

```
17540          If I Had You          Roul R(S) 52104.
17541          What'll I Do          Roul 4516, R(S) 52104.
17542          You're Driving Me      Roul R(S) 52104.
                  Crazy
17543          Always On My Mind     Roul R(S) 52104.
17544          Solitude              Roul R(S) 52104, (E)Rou 1021,
                                        (E)RE 103.
17545          I'll Never Be The     Roul R(S) 52104, (E)Rou 1021.
                  Same
17546          So Long My Love       Roul R(S) 52104.
17547          The Lonely Hours      Roul R(S) 52104, RE 105.
17548          These Foolish         Roul R(S) 52104, (E)RE 103.
                  Things
17549          Look For Me I'll      Roul R(S) 52104.
                  Be Around
17550          Friendless            Roul R(S) 52104.
17551          The Man I Love        Roul R(S) 52104, (E)Rou 1021,
                                        (E)RE 103.
```

R(S) 52104 = (E)Col 33SX 1651.

163. LALO SCHIFRIN ORCHESTRA
probably 4 tb, strings, cel, g, p, b, d, and bgo.
                    Universal Studios Chicago, Late June, 1963

```
17552          More Than You Know  Roul R(S) 52112.
17553          Something I Dreamed Roul R(S) 52112, RE 105.
                  Last Night
17554          Lazy Afternoon      Roul R(S) 52112, (E)RE 105.
17555          I Didn't Know       Roul R(S) 52112.
                  About You
```

164. LALO SCHIFRIN ORCHESTRA
probably 4 tp, 3/4 tb, 4 reeds, fl, cl, b-cl, picc, p, g, b,
and d.
                    Universal Studios, Chicago, Late June, 1963

```
17556          Just You, Just Me   Roul R(S) 52112.
17557          Thanks For The Ride Roul R(S) 52112.
```

165. LALO SCHIFRIN ORCHESTRA
probably 4 tp, 3/4 tb, 4 reeds, 2 fl, p, g, b and d.
                    Universal Studios, Chicago, Late June, 1963

```
17558          I Got Rhythm        Roul R(S) 52112,
                                      (E)Col 45DB 7500.
17559          I Wish I Were In    Roul R(S) 52112, RE 105,
                  Love Again          (E)Col 45DB 7500.
17560          This Can't Be Love  Roul R(S) 52112, RE 105.
17561          Just Married Today  Roul R(S) 52112, RE 105.
```

166. LALO SCHIFRIN ORCHESTRA
probably 4 tb, cel, p, g, b, d, bgo and strings.
                    Universal Studios, Chicago, Late June, 1963

```
17562          Come Spring         Roul R(S) 52112, (E)RE 103.
17563          Slowly              Roul R(S) 52112, RE 105,
                                      (E)RE 103.
```
R(S) 52112 = (E)Col 33SX 1697.

167.   MARTY MANNING ORCHESTRA
unknown strings, woodwinds, frhs, p, g, b, d,
and tymp/vibes/bells.

NYC, July 22, 1963

17670	'Till The End Of Time	unissued
17671	None But The Lonely Heart	unissued
17672	Night	unissued
17673	If You Are But A Dream	unissued
17693	Only	Roul 4547, R(S) 52108, RE 105, (E)Col 33SX 1645.
17694	Experience Unnecessary	unissued

Note:- 17693 and 17694 were originally 17674 and 17675 but
      changed due to conflict.
The above 6 tracks plus R(S) 52123 are available on CD 1029

168.   QUINCY JONES ORCHESTRA

Copenhagen, July, 1963

29199	He Never Mentioned Love	Merc (E)MGE 12613.
29200	Gone	Merc 72187, (E)MGE 12613.
29201	Right Or Wrong	Merc (E)MGE 12613.
29202	Show Me A Man	Merc 72187, (E)MGE 12163, (E) 20109 (S)MCL.

169.   KIRK STUART TRIO
Kirk Stuart (p), Charles Williams (b), George Hughes (d).
Tivoli, Copenhagen, 18-21 July, 1963

29209	I Feel Pretty	Merc MG 20831, (E)2EM 412.
29238	Misty	Merc MG 20831, (E)2EM 412.
29239	What Is This Thing Called Love	Merc MG 20831, (E)2EM 412, (E)Phi Son 031, T-1ST 125.
29240	Lover Man	Merc MG 20831, (E)2EM 412.
29241	Sometimes I'm Happy	Merc MG 20831, (E)2EM 412.
29242	Won't You Come Home Bill Bailey	Merc MG 20831, (E)Phi Son 031.
29243	Tenderly	Merc MG 20831.
29244	Sassy's Blues	Merc MG 20831, (E)2EM 412.
29245	Polka Dots And Moonbeams	Merc MG 20831, (E)2EM 412.
29246	I Cried For You	Merc MG 20831, (E)2EM 412.
29251	I Feel Pretty	unissued.
29252	Poor Butterfly	Merc (J).
29253	I Could Write A Book	Merc (J).
29254	Time After Time	Merc (J).
29255	All Of Me	Merc (J).*
29256	I Feel Pretty	unissued.
29257	Misty	unissued.
29258	I Hadn't Anyone 'Till You	Merc (J).

29259	I Can't Give You Anything But Love	Merc (J).*
29260	I'll Be Seeing You	Merc (J).*
29261	The Lady's In Love With You	unissued.
29262	Maria	Merc (J).*
29263	Won't You Come Home Bill Bailey	unissued.
29264	Day In, Day Out	Merc (J).*
29265	Fly Me To The Moon	Merc (J).*
29266	Baubles, Bangles And Beads	Merc (J).
29267	You're Blase	unissued.
29268	The Lady's In Love With You	Merc (J).
29269	Honeysuckle Rose	Merc (J).*
29270	What Is This Thing Called Love	Merc (J).*
29271	Lover Man	Merc (J).*
29272	I Cried For You	Merc (J).*
29273	Maria	unissued.
29274	Day In, Day Out	unissued.
29275	The More I See You	Merc (J).
29276	I Could Write A Book	unissued.
29277	Say It Isn't So	Merc (J).*
29278	The Lady's In Love With You	unissued.
29279	All Of Me	unissued.
29280	Out Of This World	unissued.
29281	Black Coffee	Merc (J).*
29282	I Cried For You	unissued.
29283	Won't You Come Home Bill Bailey	unissued.
29284	I Feel Pretty	unissued.
29285	Fly Me To the Moon	unissued.
29286	Baubles, Bangles And Beads	unissued.
29287	But Not For Me	unissued.
29288	The Lady's In Love With You	unissued
29289	What Is This Thing Called Love	unissued.
29290	Lover Man	unissued.
29291	Maria	unissued.
29292	Just One Of Those Things	Merc (J).*
29293	The More I See You	unissued.
29294	I Could Write A Book	unissued.
29295	You're Blase	unissued.
29296	Misty	unissued.
29297	On Green Dolphin Street	Merc (J).
29298	Over The Rainbow	Merc (J).*
29300	The Lady's In Love With You	unissued.
29301	Maria	unissued.

29302	Won't You Come Home Bill Bailey	unissued.
29303	Once In A While	unissued.
29304	Baubles, Bangles And Beads	unissued.
29305	Don't Blame Me	unissued.
29306	The Lady's In Love With You	unissued.
29307	Honeysuckle Rose	unissued.
29308	Won't You Come Home Bill Bailey	unissued.

MG 20831 = SR 60831, (E) 20011 (S)MCL, (E)Fontana SFJL 9963.
29199 - 29246 on Merc (J) 18PJ-1074.) except tracks
29252 - 29268 on Merc (J) 18PJ-1075. (listed as
29269 - 29298 on Merc (J) 18PJ-1076. ("unissued".
Note:- Tracks with * were issued only in Japan.
        Titled "Sassy Swings The Tivoli" SMX-7081.

170. QUINCY JONES ORCHESTRA
full string section and Svend Saaby Choir (no rhythm
section). arranged and conducted by Robert Farnon.
                              Copenhagen, Oct 12, 1963

29441	Charade	Merc MG 20882, MG 21009, SR 61009, (E) 20059 (S)MCL.
29442	It Could Happen To You	Merc MG 20882, (E) 10020 MCE.
29443	Blue Orchids	Merc MG 20882, (E) 10020 MCE.
29444	This Heart Of Mine	Merc MG 20882, (E) 10020 MCE.
29445	Then I'll Be Tired Of You	Merc MG 20882.
29446	Funny	Merc MG 20882.
29447	My Coloring Book	Merc MG 20882, (E) 10019 MCE, (E)Phi Son 031.
29448	How Beautiful Is Night	Merc MG 20882, (E) 10020 MCE.
29449	Hey There	Merc MG 20882, (E) 10019 MCE.
29450	Deep Purple	Merc MG 20882, (E) 10019 MCE.
29451	I'll Be Around	Merc MG 20882.
29452	The Days Of Wine And Roses	Merc MG 20882, MG 21009, SR 61009, (E) 10019 MCE, (E) 20059 (S)MCL.

MG 20882 = SR 60882, (E) 20014 (S)MCL, (E) 6336 225.
29441 - 29452 on Merc (J) 18PJ-1077.

171. QUINCY JONES ORCHESTRA
arranged by Billy Byers or *Claus Ogerman
                              LA, Feb 13-14, 1964

31573	How's The World Treating You	Merc 72300.
31574	My Darling, My Darling	Merc (J).
31575	Bluesette	Merc 72249, (E) 10027 MCE.
31576	You Got It Made*	Merc 72249.
31577	Make Someone Happy	Merc (J).
31578	Sole, Sole	Merc 72300.

172. FRANK FOSTER ORCHESTRA
Richard Hixon, Billy Byers, Britt Woodman, Wayne Andre,
Benny Powell (tb), Jerome Richardson (fl), Bob James (p),
Barry Galbraith (g), George Duvivier (b), Bobby Donaldson
(d), Willie Rodriguez (perc), 8 Violins.
                                          NYC, Aug 13, 1964

32598	Mr. Lucky	Merc 72334, MG 20941.
32599	The Boy From	Merc MG 20941, (E) 10032 MCE,
	Ipanema	(E)MFP MF 1107.

173. FRANK FOSTER ORCHESTRA
personnel as Aug 13, 1964 except Jimmy Cleveland, Paul
Faulise (tb) and Robert Rodriguez (b), replace Woodman,
Powell and Duvivier. Galbraith and Willie Rodriguez out.
Jose Mangual, Juan Cadavieco, Raphael Sierra (perc), added.
                                          NYC, Aug 14, 1964

33750	Quiet Nights	Merc MG 20941, (E) 10032 MCE.
	(Corcovado)*	
33751	Jive Samba	Merc MG 20941.

* strings out, (g) added.

174. FRANK FOSTER ORCHESTRA
Kai Winding, Richard Hixon, Billy Byers, Wayne Andre, Benny
Powell (tb), Jerome Richardson (fl), Bob James (p), Robert
Rodriguez (b), Bobby Donaldson, William Correa, Juan
Cadavieco, Jose Mangual, Rafael Sierra (perc), 8 violins.
                                          NYC, Aug 15, 1964

33781	A Taste Of Honey	Merc MG 20941.
33782	Shiny Stockings	Merc MG 20941.
33783	Night Song	Merc MG 20941,
		(E) 20085 (S)MCL.
33784	Stompin' At The	Merc MG 20941, (E) 6612 040.
	Savoy*	
33785	Fascinating Rhythm*	Merc MG 20941, (E) 10032 MCE.
33786	The Moment Of	Merc MG 20941, (E) 10032 MCE.
	Truth*	
33787	Tea For Two*	Merc MG 20941.

* strings out

175. FRANK FOSTER ORCHESTRA
personnel as Aug 15, 1964, except William Watrous (tb),
replaces Byers.
                                          NYC, Aug 18, 1964

33804	Fever	Merc 72334, MG 20941,
		(E)MFP MF 1107.
33805	Avalon	Merc MG 20941.

MG 20941 = SR 60941, (E) 20046 (S)MCL, (E) 6636 224.
31573 - 33805 on Merc (J) 18PJ-1078.

176. QUINCY JONES ORCHESTRA
personnel unknown. arranged Bob James.

NYC, Dec 14, 1964

| 34239 | We Almost Made It | Merc 72381. |
| 34240 | The Other Half Of Me | Merc 72381. |

177. QUINCY JONES ORCHESTRA
personnel unknown. arranged Bob James or Bill Holman.

NYC, Dec, 1964

34989	How Soon	Merc MG 21009, (E) 6619 035.
34990	Dear Heart	Merc MG 21009.
34991	Too Little Time	Merc MG 21009.
34992	Dreamsville	Merc MG 21009.
34993	Bye-Bye (From "Peter Gunn")	Merc MG 21009, (E) 20085 (S)MCL.
34994	Moon River	Merc MG 21009, (E) 6619 035.
34995	(I Love You And) Don't You Forget It	Merc MG 21009.
34996	Slow Hot Wind	Merc MG 21009, (E)Phi SON 031.
34997	It Had Better Be Tonight	Merc MG 21009.

MG 21009 = SR 61009, (E) 20059 (S)MCL.

178. BENNY CARTER ORCHESTRA
personnel unknown. produced by Quincy Jones.

circa March, 1965

| 35029 | Pawnbroker's Theme | Merc 72417, MEP 88, 830726-1. |

179. STUDIO ORCHESTRA
personnel unknown. arranged Luchi de Jesus.

NYC, Oct 20, 1965

36993	Darling	Merc 72510.
36994	I'll Never Be Lonely Again	Merc 72510.
36995	Habibi (Love Song From Sallah)	Merc MG 21069.

34239 - 36995 on Merc (J) 18PJ-1079 except 34240.

180. STUDIO ORCHESTRA
personnel unknown. arranged by Luchi de Jesus.

NYC, Nov 10. 1965

37122	Make It Easy On Yourself	Merc MG 21069.
37123	What The World Needs Now Is Love	Merc MG 21069.
37124	G.I. I Love You	unissued
37125	I Know A Place	Merc MG 21069.

181. STUDIO ORCHESTRA
personnel unknown. arrranged by Luchi de Jesus.
                                       NYC, Nov 11, 1965

37126   Little Hands   Merc MG 21069.
37127   Yesterday   Merc MG 21069.
37128   A Lover's Concerto   Merc 72543, Merc MG 21069.
37129   He Touched Me   Merc MG 21069.

182. STUDIO ORCHESTRA
personnel unknown. arranged by Luchi de Jesus.
                                       NYC, Nov 12, 1965

37148   If I Ruled The   Merc 21069.
             World
37149   Waltz For Debbie   Merc MG 21069.
37150   On A Clear Day You   Merc MG 21069.
             Can See Forever
37151   The First Thing   Merc 72543, MG 21069.
             Every Morning

MG 21069 = SR 61069, (E) 20085 (S)MCL (37126 and 148 omitted)

183. STUDIO ORCHESTRA
personnel unknown. arranged by Luchi de Jesus or Bob James*.
                                       NYC, April 7, 1966

37987   Who Can I Turn To*   Merc MG 21079, (E) 6619 035.
37988   The Shadow Of Your   Merc MG 21079, (E) 6619 035,
             Smile*   (E) 6870 661.
37989   I Should Have   Merc MG 21079, (E)Phi SON 031.
             Kissed Him More
37990   Call Me   Merc MG 21079, (E) 6619 035.

184. STUDIO ORCHESTRA
personnel unknown. arranged by Luchi de Jesus
                                       NYC, April 8, 1966

37992   With These Hands   Merc MG 21079.
37993   Dominique's   Merc MG 21079.
             Discotheque
37994   Everybody Loves   Merc 72588, MG 21079.
             Somebody
37995   What Now My Love   Merc MG 21079, (E) 6619 035.
37996   Love   Merc MG 21079.

185. STUDIO ORCHESTRA
unknown personnel. arranged by Luchi de Jesus.
                                       NYC, April 11,1965

37997   One, Two, Three   Merc 72566, MG 21079.
37998   Michelle   Merc MG 21079.
37999   Sneakin' Up On You   Merc MG 21079.

MG 21079 = SR 61079, (E) 20084 (S)MCL.
37122 - 37994 on Merc (J) 18PJ-1080 except 37124.

186. HAL MOONEY ORCHESTRA
Clark Terry, Charlie Shavers, Joe Newman, Freddie Hubbard
(tp), J.J.Johnson, Kai Winding (tb), Phil Woods, Benny
Golson (reeds), Bob James (p), and others.
arranged by Thad Jones*, J.J.Johnson**, Bob James+,
            Manny Albam++.

                              NYC, circa Jan 20-22, 1967

39352	Jim*	Merc MG 21122.
39353	The Man That Got Away+	Merc MG 21122, (E) 6619 035.
39354	My Man*	Merc MG 21122.
39355	Happiness Is Just A Thing Called Joe*	Merc MG 21122, (E) 6619 035.
		Merc MG 21122, (E) 6619 035, (E)Phi SON 031.
39356	Trouble Is A Man+	Merc MG 21122.
39357	He's Funny That Way**	Merc MG 21122.
39358	For Every Man There's A Woman**	Merc MG 21122.
39359	I'm Just Wild About Harry*	Merc MG 21122, (E)Phi SON 031.
39360	Danny Boy*	Merc MG 21122.
39361	Alfie**	Merc MG 21122, (E) 6619 035.

MG 21122 = SR 61122, (E) 20109 (S)MCL.
37995 - 39361 on Merc (J) 18PJ-1081.

187. HAL MOONEY ORCHESTRA
personnel as Jan 20-22, 1967.

                              NYC, Jan 23, 1967

39362	On The Other Side Of The Tracks**	Merc MG 21116, (E)Phi Son 031.
39364	All Alone*	Merc MG 21116, Btm 10-5516.
38365	I Want To Be Happy*	Merc MG 21116, Btm 10-5516.
38366	S'posin'++	Merc MG 21116, (E)Phi SON 031.
38369	I Had A Ball**	Merc MG 21116, (E) 6870 635.

188. HAL MOONEY ORCHESTRA
personnel as Jan 20-22, 1967.

                              NYC, Jan 24, 1967

39373	Take The "A" Train**	Merc MG 21116.
39374	I Left My Heart In San Francisco*	Merc MG 21116.
39375	The Sweetest Sounds+	Merc MG 21116, Btm 10-5516.
39376	Every Day I Have The Blues*	Merc MG 21116, Btm 10-5516, (E)Phi SON 031.
39377	Sweet Georgia Brown*	Merc MG 21116, (E)Phi SON 031.

MG 21116 = SR 61116, (E) 20105 (S)MCL.
39362 - 39377 = Merc (J) 18PJ-1082.

The Later Years

189. ANGEL "PONCHO" GATTI ORCHESTRA

San Remo, 1968

            Che Vale Per Me   (I)CDI 2019.

190. STUDIO ORCHESTRA
directed by Quincy Jones

LA, 1969

            Sun Dance   Bell 1200.

191. STUDIO ORCHESTRA
directed by Quincy Jones

LA, 1969

  9330-S-BW A Time For Love Is Bell B-832, 1202.
            Anytime

192. ERNIE WILKINS ORCHESTRA
Buddy Childers, Al Aarons, Gene Coe (tp), George Bohanon,
Benny Powell (tb), Jerome Richardson, Bill Green, Jackie
Kelso (saxes), Willie May (p), Joe Pass, Al Vescovo (g), Bob
Magnusson (b), Earl Palmer (d), Alan Estes, Jimmy Cobb (perc)
                              LA, Nov 16-20, 1971

            Imagine   Mains MST 5512, MRL 340.
            On Thinking It Over Mains MRL 340.
            Inner City Blues   Mains MST 5517, MRL 340.
            Sweet Gingerbread   Mains MST 5512, MRL 340.
              Man
            Magical Connection Mains MRL 340.
            Thats The Way I   Mains MRL 340.
              Heard It Should
              Be
            Tomorrow City   Mains MRL 340.
            Universal Prisoner Mains MRL 340.
            Trouble   Mains MRL 340.
            If Not For You   Mains MRL 340.

MRL 340 = (E) MSL 1024.

193. MICHEL LEGRAND ORCHESTRA
Buddy Childers, Chuck Findley, Conte Condoli, Gary Barone,
Al Aarons (tp), Lloyd Ulyate, Charlie Loper, Frank Rosolino,
Grover Mitchell, Bob Knight, George Roberts (tb), Tommy
Johnson (tu), Vince De Rosa, Bill Hinshaw, Art Maebe, George
Price, Sinclair Lott, Ralph Pyle, Dick Perissi, Dick Macker
(frh), Bud Shank, Pete Christlieb, Jerome Richardson, Bob
Cooper, Bill Hood, Bernie Fleischer (reeds, fl), David
Grusin, Mike Wofford, Artie Kane (keyboards), Tom Tedesco
(g), Ray Brown, Chuck Berghofer, Bob Magnusson (b), Chuck
Rainey (elec-b), Shelly Manne, John Guerin (d), Larry
Bunker (perc), Michel Legrand (arr, cond), 48 strings,
2 harps, 16 voices.

LA, April 17-20, 1971

The Summer Knows	Mains MST 5527, MRL 361.
What Are You Doing The Rest Of Your Life	Mains MST 5522, MRL 361.
Once You've Been In Love	Mains MST 5521, MRL 361.
Hands Of Time (Brian's Song)	Mains MRL 361.
I Was Born In Love With You	Mains MRL 361.
I Will Say Goodbye	Mains MRL 361.
Summer Me, Winter Me	Mains MST 5527, MRL 361.
His Eyes, Your Eyes	Mains MRL 361.
Pieces Of Dreams	Mains MST 5521, MRL 361.
Blue, Green, Grey And Gone	Mains MRL 361.

MRL 361 = (E) MSL 1006.

194. LARGE STUDIO ORCHESTRAS
conducted and arranged by Peter Matz*, Michel Legrand**,
                    Jack Elliot and Allyn Ferguson++.

LA, circa 1972

And The Feelings Good*	Mains MST 5527, MRL 379.
Just A Little Lovin'+	Mains MRL 379.
Alone Again (Naturally)*	Mains MST 5544, MRL 379.
Rainy Days And Mondays*	Mains MRL 379.
Deep In The Night**	Mains MST 5527, MRL 379.
Run To Me+	Mains MST 5544, MRL 379.
Easy Evil*	Mains MRL 379.
Promise Me*	Mains MRL 379.
Take A Love Song*	Mains MRL 379.
Greatest Show On Earth+	Mains MRL 379.
When You Think Of It*	Mains MRL 379.

MRL 379 = (E) MSL 1012, America AM 6157.

195.   WITH HER TRIO
Carl Schroeder (p), John Cianelli (b), Jimmy Cobb (d).
                    Concert "Sun Plaza Hotel", Tokyo, Sept 24, 1973

A Foggy Day	Mains MRL2-401.
Poor Butterfly	Mains MRL2-401.
The Lamp Is Low	Mains MRL2-401.
'Round Midnight	Mains MRL2-401.
Willow Weep For Me	Mains MRL2-401.
There Will Never Be Another You	Mains MRL2-401.
Misty	Mains MRL2-401.
Wave	Mains MRL2-401.
Like Someone In Love	Mains MRL2-401.
My Funny Valentine	Mains MRL2-401.
All Of Me	Mains MRL2-401.
Love Story	Mains MRL2-401.
Over The Rainbow	Mains MRL2-401.
I Could Write A Book	Mains MRL2-401.
The Nearness Of You	Mains MRL2-401.
I'll Remember April	Mains MRL2-401.
Watch What Happens	Mains MRL2-401.
Bye Bye Blackbird	Mains MRL2-401.
Rainy Days And Mondays	Mains MRL 419.
I Remember You	Mains MRL 419.
I Cried For You	Mains MRL 409, MRL 419, (E)MSL 1038.
Tenderly	Mains MRL 419.

On A Clear Day
  (You Can See
  Forever)
	Mains MRL 419.

Summertime	Mains MRL 409, MRL 419, (E)MSL 1038.
The Blues	Mains MRL 419.

There Is No
  Greater Love
	Mains MRL 409, MRL 419,
	  (E)MSL 1038.

Tonight	Mains MRL 419.

MRL2-401 = (E) MSD 401, America 6175/76.
MRL 419 = (E) MSL 1040.

196.   JIMMY ROWLES QUINTET
Al Aarons* (tp), Teddy Edwards* (ts), Jimmy Rowles (p),
Monte Budwig (b), Donald Bailey (d).
                                                LA, 1974

The Folks Who Live On The Hill	Mains MPL 404.
That Face*	Mains MPL 404.
That Sunday*	Mains MPL 404.
A House Is Not A Home	Mains MPL 404.
Frasier	Mains MST 5523, MPL 404.

                    Morning Star*   Mains MPL 404.

MPL 404 = (E) MSL 1033, (E) MSH 5005.

197. LARGE STUDIO ORCHESTRAS
conducted and arranged by Gene Page, Paul Griffin*, Ernie
Wilkins**, Michel Legrand+, Wade Marcus++.

                                            LA, 1974

                    Love Don't Live   Mains MRL 412.
                      Here Any More
                    That'll Be Johnny   Mains MRL 412.
                    Right In The Next   Mains MRL 412.
                      Room
                    I Need You More   Mains MRL 412.
                      Than Ever Now
                    Do Away With April   Mains MRL 412.
                    Got To Go See If I   Mains MRL 412.
                      Can't Get Daddy
                      To Come Back Home
                    Send In The Clowns* Mains MST 5541, MRL 412.
                    On Thinking It   Mains MRL 412.
                      Over**
                    Wave+   Mains MRL 412.
                    Frasier++   Mains MRL 412.

MRL 412 = (E) MSL 1039.

198. WITH HER TRIO
Sarah Vaughan (vcl, p), Carl Schroeder (p), Robert
Magnusson (b), Jimmy Cobb (d).
                    Jazz Jamboree '75, Warsaw, Oct 24, 1975

                    The Man I Love   unissued.
                    /Tea For Two
                    I Got It Bad And   unissued.
                      That Ain't Good
                    On A Clear Day   (P)Pronit SX 0605.
                      (You Can See
                      Forever)
                    Misty   unissued.
                    A Foggy Day   (P)Pronit SX 0605.
                    'Round Midnight   (P)Pronit SX 0605.
                    Close To You   (P)Pronit SX 0605.
                    What Are You Doing   (P)Pronit SX 0605.
                      The Rest Of Your
                      Life
                    Sassy's Blues   (P)Pronit SX 0605.
                    The Nearness Of You (P)Pronit SX 0605.
                    Just A Gigolo   unissued.
                    My Funny Valentine   (P)Pronit SX 0605.
                      /Tenderly
                    Bill Bailey, Won't   (P)Pronit SX 0605.
                      You Please Come
                      Home
Note:- all above titles are included in a privately issued
      cassette (P) "Jazz Greats" SJG 12.

199.   AIRMEN OF NOTE ORCHESTRA
CMSgt. Dave Napier (director, reeds), Sgts. Ernie Hensley,
Gene Gaydos, John Dodge, Roger Hogan, Tim Eyerman (reeds),
Sgts. Ken Smukal, Jim Lay, Dick Perry, Larry Trautman (tp),
Sgts. Dave Steinmeyer, Mike Smukal, Lee Robertson, Paul
Rawlins (or Dave Boyle) (tb), Sgt. Gil Cray (p), Sgt. Rick
Whitehead (g), Sgt. Brent McKesson (b), Dave Palamar (d).
arranged by Benny Carter, Bobby Sherwood*, Dick Hazald+.
                                        Washington DC, 1976

         Love Touches Your   A of N AF 33175.
           Heart*
         My Funny Valentine   A of N AF 33175.
         Misty+   A of N AF 33175.
         There Will Never   A of N AF 33175.
           Be Another You

200.   LARGE STUDIO ORCHESTRA
Lee Ritenour, Dean Parks, Louis Shelton (g), David Paich,
Marty Paich, Mike Lang (keyboards), Davis Hungate (p), Jeff
Porcaro (perc, d), Bobbye Hall, Joe Porcaro, Steve Forman
(perc), Steve Porcaro (synth), Jean "Toots" Thielemans (harm)
John Smith* (ts), Bob Magnusson** (b), Billy Thetford (lead),
Perry Morgan, Jim Gilstrap (background singers), Sid Sharp
(concert master, strings), Marty and David Paich (rhythm,
horn and strings arrangers).
Davlen Sound Studios, Universal City, California, circa 1977

34039	Something	Atl SD 16037.
34040	Honey Pie-64	unissued.
34041	Come Together*	Atl SD 16037.
34042	The Long And Winding Road	Atl SD 16037.
34043	Oh Darling	unissued.
34044	Fool On A Hill	Atl SD 16037.+
34045	And I Love Him	Atl SD 16037.
34046	Blackbird	Atl SD 16037.
34047	Here, There And Everywhere	Atl SD 16037.
34048	You Never Give Me Your Money**	Atl SD 16037.
34049	Golden Slumbers	unissued.
34050	Eleanor Rigby	Atl SD 16037.
34051	I Want You (She's So Heavy)*	Atl SD 16037.
34052	Get Back	Atl SD 16037.+
34053	Yesterday	Atl SD 16037.
34054	Hey Jude	Atl SD 16037.
39044	Fool On A Hill	Atl 3835.+
39045	Get Back	Atl 3835.+

+these are presumably edited versions with new master number.

201.   AIRMEN OF NOTE WITH HER TRIO
probably similar personnel as 1976 recording plus Carl
Schroeder (p), Walter Booker (b), Jimmy Cobb (d).
                    Broadcast, Washington DC, March 6, 1977

```
                There Will Never Be
                    Another You
                Feelings (trio only)
                East Of The Sun (b, only)
                Golden Slumbers
                Watch What Happens
                Misty
                The Lamp Is Low
                Here, There And
                    Everywhere
                Sassy's Blues (trio only)
                Send In The Clowns (trio only)
                What Are You Doing
                    The Rest Of Your
                    Life
                Tenderly
```

202. AIRMEN OF NOTE ORCHESTRA
probably similar personnel to 1976 recording

                                                circa 1977

```
                Bright Lights And   A of N Program No. 303.
                    You
                The Lamp Is Low     A of N Program No. 303.
                What Are You Doing  A of N Program No. 303.
                    The Rest Of Your
                    Life
                There Will Never    A of N Program No. 397.
                    Be Another You
                Take The "A" Train  A of N Program No. 397.
                Misty               A of N Program No. 397.
                Love Touches        A of N Program No. 447.
                    Your Heart
                Where Do I Begin    A of N Program No. 447.
                My Funny Valentine  A of N Program No. 447.
```

203. WITH HER TRIO
Carl Schroeder (p), Walter Booker (b), Jimmy Cobb (d).
            Live, Ronnie Scott Club, London, June 10/11, 1977

```
                Here's That Rainy   (E)Pye NSPL 18544.
                    Day
                Like Someone In     (E)Pye NSPL 18544, 5008.
                    Love
                Feelings            (E)Pye NSPL 18544.
                I'll Remember April (E)Pye NSPL 18544.
                Sophisticated Lady  (E)Pye NSPL 18544.
                If You Could See    (E)Pye NSPL 18544.
                    Me Now
                Start Believing Me  (E)Pye NSPL 18544.
                    Now
                My Funny Valentine  (E)Pye NSPL 18544.
                A Foggy Day         (E)Pye NSPL 18544.
                Send In The Clowns  (E)Pye NSPL 18544.
                Tenderly            (E)Pye NSPL 18544.
```

204. WITH HER TRIO
personnel as June 10/11 1977
                    Live, Ronnie Scott Club, London, June, 1977

```
        The Man I Love        (E)Pye N 103.
        Passing Strangers     (E)Pye N 103.
        Gershwin Medley:-      (E)Pye N 103.
          But Not For Me/Love Is Here To Stay/
          Embraceable You/ Someone To Watch
          Over Me
        Blue Skies            (E)Pye N 103.
        The More I See You     (E)Pye N 103.
        Early Autumn          (E)Pye N 103.
        On A Clear Day You     (E)Pye N 103.
          Can See Forever
        Everything Must        (E)Pye N 103,
          Change              (E)Debut Deb X 18.
        I Cried For You        (E)Pye N 103.
```

205. VARIOUS STUDIO GROUPS
arranged by Edson Frederico (p).
                Rio De Janeiro, Oct 31, Nov 3,4,5 and 7, 1977
a) Milton Nascimento (g, vcl), Jose Roberto Bertrami
   (fender p), Novelli (fender b), Nelson Angelo (fender g),
   Roberto Silva* (d), Danilo Caymmi, Paulo Jobim (fl), Chico
   Batera, Arivoldo (perc).
b) Jose Roberto Bertami (fender p), Sergio Barroso= or
   Claudio Bertrami++ (b), Helio Delmiro (g), Chico Batera,
   Ariovaldo (perc), Mauricio Einhorn+ (harm), Wilson Das
   Neves (d), Dorival Caymmi** (vcl).
c) Tom Jobim (yamaha p), Jose Roberto Bertrami (fender p),
   Helio Delmiro (g), Wilson Das Neves (d), Sergio Barroso
   (b), Chico Batera, Ariovaldo (perc).
d) probably either a), b), or c).

```
60340 754   Someone To Light      (Br)RCA 110-0018.
              Up My Life c)
60340 797   Courage a)            Pablo 2312-101,
                                  (Br)RCA 110-0018.
60340 835   Roses And Roses       Pablo 2312-101,
              b),**               (Br)RCA 110-0018.
60340 878   A Little Tear b),=    Pablo 2312-101,
                                  (Br)RCA 110-0018.
60340 916   The Day It Rained     Pablo 2312-101,
              b),+,++,            (Br)RCA 110-0018.
              (omit perc)
60340 959   Triste c)            Pablo 2312-101,
                                  (Br)RCA 110-0018.
60340 991   If You Went Away      Pablo 2312-101,
              b),=                (Br)RCA 110-0018.
60341 076   Bridges a),*          (Br)RCA 110-0018.
60341 262   I Live To Love You    Pablo 2312-101,
              (p, only)           (Br)RCA 110-0018.
            Vera Cruz d)         Pablo 2312-101.
            The Face I Love d)   Pablo 2312-101.
            Cantador d)          Pablo 2312 101.
```

206. COUNT BASIE ORCHESTRA
Waymon Reed, Lyn Biviano, Sonny Cohn, Pete Minger (tp), Bill
Hughes, Mel Wanzo, Fred Welsey, Dennis Wilson (tb), Danny
Turner, Bobby Plater, Eric Dixon, Kenny King, Charlie Fowkles
(saxes), Count Basie (p, ldr), Milt Jackson (vib), Freddy
Green (g), John Clayton (b), Butch Miles (d).

Hollywood, Jan 18, 1978

Lena And Lennie   Pablo 2310 832.

Note:- Not a vocal feature, Sarah joins the sax section with
       wordless "vocal" throughout.

207. WITH ALLSTAR QUARTET
Oscar Peterson (p), Joe Pass (g), Ray Brown (b), Louis
Bellson (d).

Hollywood, April 25, 1978

I've Got The World On A String	Pablo 2310 821, 2310 885.
Midnight Sun	Pablo 2310 821, 2310 885.
How Long Has This Been Going On	Pablo 2310 821.
You're Blase	Pablo 2310 821, 2310 885.
Easy Living	Pablo 2310 821.
More Than You Know	Pablo 2310 821.
My Old Flame	Pablo 2310 821.
Teach Me Tonight	Pablo 2310 821.
Body And Soul	Pablo 2310 821.
When Your Lover Has Gone	Pablo 2310 821.

208. STUDIO ORCHESTRA PLUS SUB-GROUPS
Jimmy Rowles or Mike Wofford* (p), Joe Pass (g), Andy
Simpkins (b), Grady Tate (d). Solos by Waymon Reed**
(t, flgh), J.J.Johnson+ (tb), Frank Wess++ (ts, fl), Zoot
Sims= (ts), plus others, Billy Byers (arr, big band numbers).

Hollywood, Aug 15/16, 1979

I'm Just A Lucky So And So**	Pablo 2312 111.
Solitude+	Pablo 2312 111.
I Didn't Know About You	Pablo 2312 111.
All Too Soon++	Pablo 2312 111.
Sophisticated Lady++	Pablo 2312 111.
Day Dream=	Pablo 2312 111.
What Am I Here For**	Pablo 2312 116.
I Ain't Got Nothing But The Blues*	Pablo 2312 116.
Everything But You*	Pablo 2312 116.
Prelude To A Kiss	Pablo 2312 116.

209. STUDIO ORCHESTRA PLUS SUB-GROUPS
Mike Wofford (p), Bucky Pizzarelli (g), Andy Simpkins (b),
Grady Tate (d). Solos by Frank Foster* (ts), Waymon Reed**
(t, flgh), Frank Wess++ (fl), Eddie "Cleanhead" Vinson+
(as, vcl), and others.

NYC, Sept 12/13, 1979

In A Sentimental Mood	Pablo 2312 111, 2312 885.
I Let A Song Go Out Of My Heart*	Pablo 2312 111.

```
        Lush Life           Pablo 2312 111, 2312 885.
        In A Mellow Tone*    Pablo 2312 111.
        Black Butterfly+     Pablo 2312 116.
        Tonight I Shall      Pablo 2312 116.
          Sleep++
        I Got It Bad And     Pablo 2312 116.
          That Ain't Good**
        It Don't Mean A      Pablo 2312 116.
          Thing
```

Lloyd Glenn (p), Pee Wee Clayton (g), Bill Walker (b),
Charles Randell (d), replace Wofford, Pizzarelli, Simpkins
and Tate.

```
        Rocks In My Bed+     Pablo 2312 116.
```

Roy McCurdy (d) replaces Randell.

```
        Chelsea Bridge       Pablo 2312 116.
        Mood Indigo**        Pablo 2312 116.
```

210. BRAZILIAN GROUP
Native Rhythm Section and Singers, Helio Delmiro (g, elec g),
Andy Simpkins (b), Wilson Das Neves or Grady Tate* (d),
Edson Fredrico (arr).
                              Rio De Janeiro, Oct 1-5, 1979

```
60999 05 5 Bonita           Pablo 2312 125.
60999 06 3 Dindi            Pablo 2312 125, 2312 885.
60999 07 1 Double Rainbow*  Pablo 2312 125.
60999 08 0 Copacabana       Pablo 2312 125.
60999 13 6 To Say Goodbye   Pablo 2312 125.
60999 14 4 Gentle Rain      Pablo 2312 125.
60999 15 2 Dreamer          Pablo 2312 125.
60999 17 9 Tete             Pablo 2312 125.
60999 20 9 The Smiling Hour Pablo 2312 125.
```

2312 125 = (E)Philips 6485 202 and (Br)Philips 6485 202.
           (title "Exclusivamente Brazil-Sarah Vaughan).

211. COUNT BASIE ORCHESTRA AND HER TRIO
Sonny Cohn, Frank Szabo, Bob Summers, Dale Carley (tp),
Mitchell "Booty" Wood*, Bill Hughes, Dennis Wilson, Grover
Mitchell (tb), Kenny Hing**, Eric Dixon, Bobby Plater, Johnny
Wilson (saxes), George Gaffney (p), Freddie Green (g), Andy
Simpkins (b), Harold Jones (d).
Sam Nestico or Allyn Ferguson+ (arr).
                              Hollywood, Feb 16 and 18, 1981

```
        I Got A Right To     Pablo 2312 130, 2310 885.
          Sing The Blues*
        Just Friends         Pablo 2312 130.
        Ill Wind             Pablo 2312 130.
        If You Could See     Pablo 2312 130.
          Me Now+
        I Hadn't Anyone      Pablo 2312 130.
          'Till You
        Send In The Clowns   Pablo 2312 130.
```

All The Things You Are**	Pablo 2312 130.
Indian Summer	Pablo 2312 130.
When Your Lover Has Gone	Pablo 2312 130.
From This Moment On	Pablo 2312 130, 2310 885.

212. STUDIO ORCHESTRA.
arranged and conducted by Al Capps.

                                                      LA, May 14, 1981

| ZCA 1447 | Love Theme From "Sharkey's Machine" | Warner BSK 3652, (E) 104105. |

213. STUDIO ORCHESTRA, DUET WITH JOE WILLIAMS (vcl).
arranged and conducted by Al Capps.

                                                      LA, Sept 14, 1981

| ZCA 1452 | Before You | Warner BSK 3652, (E) 104105. |

214. LOS ANGELES PHILHARMONIC ORCHESTRA AND HER TRIO.
Michael Tilson Thomas (dir, arr**, p*), Marty Paich (arr),
George Gaffney (p), Andy Simpkins (b), Harold Jones (d).
                    Dorothy Chandler Auditorium, LA, Feb 1/2,1982

Medley:- Summertime/Ain't Necessarily So/ I Loves You Porgy	CBS 37277, (E)CBS 42516.
Medley:- But Not For Me/ Love Is Here To Stay/Embraceable You/Someone To Watch Over Me	CBS 37277.
Sweet And Lowdown*	CBS 37277.
Fascinating Rhythm	CBS 37277.
Do It Again*	CBS 37277.
My Man's Gone Now	CBS 37277.
The Man I Love**	CBS 37277.
Medley:- Nice Work If You Can Get It/They Can't Take That Away From Me/ 'S Wonderful/ Swanee/Strike Up The Band	CBS 37277.
Encore:- I've Got A Crush On You/A Foggy Day	CBS 37277.

CBS 37277 = (E)CBS 73650.

215. WITH HER QUARTET
Roland Hanna (p), Joe Pass (g), Andy Simpkins (b), Harold
Jones (d).
Hollywood, March 1/2, 1982

I Didn't Know What Time It Was	Pablo 2312 137.
That's All	Pablo 2312 137.
Autumn Leaves	Pablo 2312 137.
Love Dance	Pablo 2312 137.
The Island	Pablo 2312 137.
In Love In Vain	Pablo 2312 137.
Seasons	Pablo 2312 137.
You Are Too Beautiful	Pablo 2312 137.

216. BARRY MANILOW SEXTET.
Gerry Mulligan (bar), Barry Manilow (p, ldr, vcl), Mundell
Lowe (g), Bill Mays (rhodes), George Duvivier (b), Shelly
Manne (d).
Westlake Studio, Hollywood, April 19,1984

Blue	Arista 8254, (E) 206496.

217. STUDIO ORCHESTRA
Lalo Shifrin (cond), Benny Bailey, Rick Kiefer, Idrees
Sulieman, Art Farmer, Rolf Ericson, Klaus Osterloh (tp),
Bart Van Lier, Henning Berg, Otto Bredl, Jiggs Wigham, Erik
Van Lier (tb), Ferdinand Povel, Tony Coe, Sal Nistico,
Gianni Basso, Sahib Shihab (saxes, woodwinds), Bobby Scott
or Francy Boland (p), Jimmy Wood, Chris Lawrence (b), Sadi,
Hans-Joachim Schacht (perc), Thomas Baumartel, Andrea Joy,
Ludwig Raft, Hubert Stale (fhr), Claus Boden, Andreas
Bossler, Bern Holz, Karin Levin, Jonel Radonici, Michel
Riessler, Harald Rodde, Markus Rodde, Markus Strohmeyer
(woodwinds), 26 strings, Cary Wilson, Ken Evans, Joan Baxter,
Lee Gibson, Norma Winstone (chorus), Francy Boland (arr).
Dusseldorf, West Germany, June 30, 1984

The Mystery Of Man	Jazzletter JLR-1.
The Actor	Jazzletter JLR-1.
Girl Disappointed In Love	Jazzletter JLR-1.
The Madeleine	Jazzletter JLR-1.
The Children	Jazzletter JLR-1.
The Armaments Worker	Jazzletter JLR-1.
Let It Live	Jazzletter JLR-1.

218. LONDON SYMPHONY ORCHESTRA
Jonathan Tunick (dir).
Henry Wood Hall, London, Jan 27/31, 1986
Happy Talk	CBS 42205, (E) 42205.
Bali Ha'i	CBS 42205, (E) 42205.

219.   STUDIO ORCHESTRA
George Duke (keyboards), Dan Huff, Dori Caymmi (g), Alphonso
Johnson (b), Paulinho Da Costa (perc), 15 violins, 4 celli,
harp.   Solos:- Hubert Laws (fl*), Tom Scott (lyricon**, ts+),
Ernie Watts (as++), Marcio Montarroyos (fhn=, tp==), Chuck
Domanico (b***), Siedah, Gracinha Leporace, Kate Markowitz
(background vocals+++), Dori Caymmi (arr), Milton Nascimento
(vcl===),(recorded in Rio De Janeiro).
produced by Sergio Mendes.
  A and M Studios and Motown/Hitsville Studios, Jan/Feb, 1987

Make This City Ours	CBS 42519.
Tonight +==	
Romance=	CBS 42519.
Love And Passion**	CBS 42519.
===	
So Many Stars	CBS 42519.
Photograph***	CBS 42519.
Nothing Will Be As	CBS 42519.
It Was++	
It's Simple	CBS 42519.
Obsession*	CBS 42519.
Wanting More	CBS 42519.
Your Smile===	CBS 42519.

CBS 42519 = (E)CBS 460156 1.

220.   MORMON TABERNACLE CHOIR AND UTAH SYMPHONY ORCHESTRA,
       DUET WITH SAMUEL RAMSEY (vcl).*

                                                  Summer, 1988

Bless This Day*	Hallmark Cards PR 9732.
(orch only)	
Medley:-	Hallmark Cards PR 9732.
White Christmas/	
Happy Holiday/	
White Christmas	
What Child Is This	Hallmark Cards PR 9732.

221.   QUINCY JONES GROUPS
a) Jerry Hey (tp), Larry Williams (sax), Bill Summers (perc).
Solos by Dizzy Gillespie, Miles Davis (tp), James Moody (as),
George Benson (g), Josef Zawinul (synth), Ella Fitzgerald
(vcl).
b) Ian Prince, Larry Williams (keyboards), Nathan East (b),
Jerry Hey, Gary Grant (tp),Larry Williams (sax), Bill
Reichenbach (tb).
Solos by Dizzy Gillespie, Miles Davis (tp), James Moody (as),
George Benson (g), Ella Fitzgerald (vcl).
c) Greg Phillinganes, Ian Price, David Paich (keyboards),
Paulinho Da Costa (perc).
Solos by Gerald Albright (as), George Benson (g), George Duke
(fender rhodes), Herbie Hancock (keyboards), Take 6 (vcl).
d) Bobby McFerrin (perc, b), Take 6, Edie Lehman, (vcl).
featured vocalists and scat solos*, Ella Fitzgerald*, Siedah
Garrett, Al Jarreau, Bobby McFerrin*,
                     "Colossus", Oceanway Record One, LA, 1989

```
Jazz Corner Of The   Q West 9 26020-1.
  Word a)
Birdland b)          Q West 9 26020-1.
Septembro            Q West 9 26020-1.
  (Brazilian
  Lovesong) c)
Wee B. Doooinit      Q West 9 26020-1.
  (A Cappela
  Party) d)
```

Q West 926020 = (E) WEA K9260202

Sarah was due to make a recording for Quincy Jones on April 2, 1990 in LA. Sarah had told Quincy "Don't worry Q. I sing real good when I lay down." Sarah was too ill to perform that last "gig"; she passed away the following day.

II
SONG TITLES
AND COMPOSERS

III
RECORD COMPANY ISSUES

Major Record Companies' LPs

AIRMEN OF NOTE

AF 33175   THE AIRMEN OF NOTE AND SARAH VAUGHAN
                Love Touches Your Heart
                My Funny Valentine
                Misty

303   Bright Lights And You
                The Lamp Is Low
                What Are You Doing The Rest Of Your Life?

397   There Will Never Be Another You
                Take The "A" Train
                Misty

447   Love Touches Your Heart
                Where Do I Begin? (Love Story)
                My Funny Valentine

AFRS

25   After Hours
                Time To Go
                A City Called Heaven
                Ave Maria

ATLANTIC

SD 16037   SONGS OF THE BEATLES
CD 16037-2   Get Back
                And I Love Her
                Eleanor Rigby
                Fool On The Hill
                You Never Give Me Your Money
                Come Together
                I Want You
                Blackbird
                Something
                Here,There And Everywhere
                The Long And Winding Road

                    Yesterday
                    Hey Jude

ARISTA

206496   PARADISE CAFE - 2AM
                    Blues

BELL

1200   BOB AND CAROL AND TED AND ALICE Soundtrack
                    Sundance

1201   CACTUS FLOWER Soundtrack
                    The Time For Love Is Anytime

CANADIAN AMERICAN

CALP 1003   MURDER INCORPORATED Soundtrack
                    The Awakening
                    Fan My Brow

COLUMBIA/CBS/HARMONY/PHILIPS (E)

CL 660   AFTER HOURS
                    After Hours
                    Street Of Dreams
                    You Taught Me To Love Again
                    You're Mine You
                    My Reverie
                    Summertime
                    Black Coffee
                    Thinking Of You
                    I Cried For You
                    Perdido
                    Deep Purple
                    Just Friends

FCPA 730   SUMMERTIME
                    Black Coffee
                    I Cried For You
                    Perdido
                    Summertime
                    The Nearness Of You
                    Mean To Me

CL 745   SARAH VAUGHAN IN HI-FI
CPS EN 13084   East Of The Sun
                    Nice Work If You Can Get It
                    Pinky
                    The Nearness Of You
                    Come Rain Or Come Shine
                    Mean To Me
                    It Might As Well Be Spring
                    Can't Get Out Of This Mood
                    Spring Will Be A Little Late This Year
                    Ooh,What-cha Doin' To Me
                    Goodnight My Love
                    Ain't Misbehavin'

CL 777 $64,OOO JAZZ
                          Perdido

CL 914   LINGER AWHILE
BBL 7165 (E)   Linger Awhile
                          These Things I Offer You
                          My Tormented Heart
                          Lonely Girl
                          Mighty Lonesome Feeling
                          Blues Serenade
                          A Lover's Quarrel
                          I Confess
                          Don't Be Afraid
                          I'm Crazy To Love You
                          Just A Moment More
                          Sinner Or Saint

CSP 14364   LINGER AWHILE
                          As You Desire Me
                          These Things I Offer You
                          Tonight I Shall Sleep
                          While You Are Gone
                          I'll Know
                          Nice Work If You Can Get It
                          Linger Awhile
                          If Someone Had Told Me
                          Give Me A Song With A Beautiful Melody
                          Time
                          East Of The Sun
                          A Miracle Happened

CL 6133   SARAH VAUGHAN
                          East Of The Sun
                          Nice Work If You Can Get It
                          Come Rain Or Come Shine
                          Mean To Me
                          It Might As Well Be Spring
                          Can't Get Out Of This Mood
                          Goodnight My Love
                          Ain't Misbehavin'

CL 6233   POPULAR FAVOURITES
                          My Tormented Heart

CBS 54303   ELLA, BILLIE, LENA AND SARAH
BBL 8115 (E)   Time
                          Sinner And Saint

BBL 7082 (E)   SARAH VAUGHAN
                          Nice Work If You Can Get It
                          Black Coffee
                          I Cried For You
                          Just Friends
                          You're Mine You
                          You Taught Me To Love Again
                          The Nearness Of You
                          Summertime
                          Linger Awhile
                          Come Rain Or Shine

Ooh What-cha Doin' To Me
As You Desire Me

54303 (E)   SARAH,BILLIE,LENA AND ELLA
                   Nice Work If You Can Get It
                   East Of The Sun
                   Ain't Misbehavin'
                   Goodnight My Love

C2-44165   THE DIVINE SARAH VAUGHAN
CD 465597   The CBS Years 1949-1953
                   Black Coffee
                   While You Are Gone
                   You Taught Me To Love Again
                   Just Friends
                   I Cried For You
                   You're Mine You
                   I'm Crazy To Love You
                   Summertime
                   The Nearness Of You
                   Ain't Misbehavin'
                   Goodnight My Love
                   Can't Get Out Of This Mood
                   It Might As Well Be Spring
                   Mean To Me
                   Come Rain Or Come Shine
                   Nice Work If You Can Get It
                   East Of The Sun
                   Thinking Of You
                   Perdido
                   I'll Know
                   Deep Purple
                   My Reverie
                   After Hours
                   Pinky
                   Street Of Dreams
                   Spring Will Be A Little Late This Year
                   Blues Serenade
                   Ooh What-cha Doin' To Me

6300 039 (E)   16 STAR TRACKS OF THE SIXTIES
                   Passing Strangers

66403 (E)   JAZZ ANTHOLOGY
                   Nice Work If You Can Get It

67203 (E)   STARS OF THE APOLLO
                   Ain't Misbehavin'

6612 040 (E)   TOUCH OF CLASS
                   Stompin' At The Savoy
                   Passing Strangers

6612 055 (E)   EVERGREEN HIT PARADE
                   Passing Strangers

6612 056 (E)   TOUCH MORE CLASS
                   Embraceable You

65329 (Eu)	NEW YORK SCENE OF THE 40's FROM BOP TO COOL
	It Might As Well Be Spring
	Nice Work If You Can Get It
	Mean To Me
	Ain't Misbehavin'
21114 (Eu)	SUMMERTIME
	Nice Work If You Can Get It
	East Of The Sun
	Mean To Me
	Come Rain Or Come Shine
	Can't Get Out Of This Mood
	It Might As Well Be Spring
	Ain't Misbehavin'
	Goodnight My Love
	Perdido
	Pinky
	I Cried For You
	The Nearness Of You
	Just Friends
	Ooh What-cha Doin' To Me
	Summertime
	Black Coffeee
	Thinking Of You
CBS 37277	GERSHWIN LIVE
73650 (E)	Medley;-Summertime
CD MK 37277	Ain't Necessarily So
	I Loves You,Porgy
	Medley;-But Not For Me
	Love Is Here To Stay
	Embraceable You
	Someone To Watch Over Me
	Sweet And Lowdown
	Fascinating Rhythm
	Do It Again
	My Man's Gone Now
	The Man I Love
	Medley;-Nice Work If You Can Get It
	They Can't Take That Away From Me
	'S Wonderful
	Swanee
	Strike Up The Band
	Medley;-I've Got A Crush On You
	A Foggy Day
CBS 42515 (E)	CLASSICAL GERSHWIN
	Medley;-Summertime
	Ain't Necessarily So
	I Loves You Porgy
CBS 42205	SOUTH PACIFIC
42205 (E)	Happy Talk
CD MK 42205	Bali Ha'i
CBS 42519	BRAZILIAN ROMANCE
460156 1 (E)	Make This City Ours Tonight
CD MK 42519	Romance
	Love And Passion

So Many Stars
Photograph
Nothing Will Be As It Was
It's Simple
Obsession
Wanting More
Your Smile

HARMONY

HL 7125   BILLIE, ELLA, LENA, SARAH!
Nice Work If You Can Get It
Ain't Misbehavin'
Goodnight My Love

HL 7158   THE GREAT SARAH VAUGHAN
I'll Know
You Say You Care
If Someone Had Told Me
Bianca
De Gas Pipe She Is Leakin' Joe
As You Desire Me
A Miracle Happened
Tonight I Shall Sleep
Time
That Lucky Old Sun

HL 7208   SARAH VAUGHAN FAVORITES
P 13517   Corner To Corner
Whippa-Whippa-Woo
Our Very Own
Time To Go
Fool's Paradise
Vanity
I Ran All The Way Home
Say You'll Wait For Me
A City Called Heaven
Ave Maria

HL 7255   GREATEST HITS
As You Desire Me

HL 7277   MORE GOLDEN HITS
titles not known

HL 11318   DEEP PURPLE
East Of The Sun
I Cried For You
Summertime
As You Desire Me
Deep Purple
Come Rain Or Come Shine
Linger Awhile
Just Friends
Thinking Of You

EUROJAZZ (I)

EJ 1002 (I)   WITH DIZZY GILLESPIE 1954
                   Embraceable You

EJ 1019 (I)   WITH CLARK TERRY QUARTET
                   Scat Blues

HARMONY CARDS

629   CAROLS OF CHRISTMAS
                   Bless This Day
                   Medley;-White Christmas
                            Happy Holiday
                   What Child Is This

JAZZ LETTER

JRL-1   LET IT LIVE
                   The Mystery Of Man
                   The Actor
                   Girl Disappointed In Love
                   The Madeleine
                   The Children
                   The Armaments Worker
                   Let It Live

KINGS OF JAZZ (I)

KLJ 20036 (I)   GREAT LADIES AT THEIR RARE OF ALL RAREST
                       PERFORMANCES
                   Everything I Have Is Yours
                   I Get A Kick Out Of You
                   Tenderly

MAINSTREAM

340   A TIME IN MY LIFE
CD MDCD 704   Sweet Gingerbread Man
plus Run To Me   Imagine
and Easy Evil   Magical Connection
                   Inner City Blues
                   Universal Prisoner
                   That's The Way I Heard It Should Be
                   Tomorrow City
                   If Not For You
                   On Thinking It Over
                   Trouble

361   SARAH VAUGHAN WITH MICHEL LEGRAND
MSL 1006 (E)   The Summer Knows
CD MDCD 703   What Are You Doing The Rest Of Your Life
plus Wave and   Once You've Been In Love
Deep In The   Hands Of Time
Night   I Was Born To Love You
                   I Will Say Goodbye
                   Summer Me,Winter Me
                   His Eyes,Your Eyes
                   Pieces Of Dreams

Blue,Green,Grey And Gone

379 MSL 1021 (E)	**FEELIN' GOOD** Alone Again (Naturally) Easy Evil When You Think Of It Take A Love Song And The Feelings Good Promise Me Rainy Days And Mondays Deep In The Night Run To Me The Greatest Show On Earth Just A Little Lovin'
404 MSL 1033 (E)	**SARAH VAUGHAN AND JIMMY ROWLES** The Folks Who Live On The Hill That Face That Sunday A House Is Not A Home Frasier (The Sensuous Lion) Morning Star
409 MSL 1038 (E)	**BILLIE HOLIDAY REVISITED** Summertime. There Is No Greater Love I Cried For You
412 MSL 1039 (E)	**SEND IN THE CLOWNS** Love Don't Live Here Anymore That'll Be Johnny Right In The Next Room I Need You More Than Ever Now On Thinking It Over Do Away With April Wave Got To See If I Can't Get Daddy To Come Back Home Frasier (The Sensuous Lion) Send In The Clowns
2-401 MSD 4001 (E) CD MDCD 701 less last 4 titles	**SARAH VAUGHAN LIVE IN JAPAN** A Foggy Day Poor Butterfly The Lamp Is Low 'Round Midnight Willow Weep For Me There Will Never Be Another You Misty Wave Like Someone In Love My Funny Valentine All Of Me Love Story Over The Rainbow I Could Write A Book The Nearness Of You I'll Remember April Watch What Happens

Bye Bye Blackbird

419	MORE SARAH VAUGHAN LIVE IN JAPAN
MSL 1040 (E)	Rainy Days And Mondays
CD MDCD 702	I Cried For You
plus last 4	On A Clear Day You Can See Forever
titles from	I Remember You
above	Tonight,Tonight
	Tenderly
	There Is No Greater Love
	Summertime
	The Blues

MERCURY/EMARCY

MG 20094	SARAH VAUGHAN AT THE BLUE NOTE
MPT 7503 (E)*	The Touch Of Your Lips
	'S Wonderful
	Tenderly
	It's Magic
	Honey
	Let's Put Out The Light And Go To Sleep
	I'm In The Mood For Love
	I Don't Know Why
	Paradise
	Time On My Hands
	Gimme A Little Kiss
	Make Yourself Comfortable

* Released In Britain As "Make Yourself Comfortable"

MG 20133	SWINGIN' FOR THE KING
	Sometimes I'm Happy

MG 20219	WONDERFUL SARAH
MPL 6532 (E)	Mr. Wonderful
CD 826333-2	I Wanna Play House
	My One And Only Love
	Oh Yeah
	And This Is My Beloved
	Whatever Lola Wants
	The Other Woman
	Experience Unnecessary
	Johnny Be Smart
	Old Devil Moon
	It's Easy To Remember
	Idle Gossip

MG 20223	IN A ROMANTIC MOOD
MPL 6540 (E)	It Happened Again
	You Ought To Have A Wife
	Slowly With Feeling
	Exactly Like You
	How Important Can It Be
	Fabulous Character
	C'est La Vie
	Never
	The Edge Of The Sea
	Waltzing Down The Aisle

Don't Let Me Love You
The Second Time

MG 20244	GREAT SONGS FROM HIT SHOWS Vol.1
SR 60041	A Tree In The Park
MPL 6522 (E)	Little Girl Blue
CMS 18019 (E)	Comes Love
MMC 14024 (E)	But Not For Me
	My Darling, My Darling
	Lucky In Love
	Autumn In New York
	It Never Entered My Mind
	If This Isn't Love
	The Touch Of Your Hand
	Homework
	Bewitched

MG 20245	GREAT SONGS FROM HIT SHOWS Vol.2
SR 60078	Dancing In The Dark
MPL 6523 (E)	September Song
CMS 18023 (E)	A Ship Without A Sail
MMC 14026 (E)	Lost In The Stars
	It's Got To Be Love
	All The Things You Are
	Poor Butterfly
	Let's Take An Old Fashioned Walk
	My Heart Stood Still
	He's Only Wonderful
	They Say It's Wonderful
	My Ship

MG 20287	FIRE DOWN BELOW
	The Banana Boat Song

MG 20310	SARAH VAUGHAN SINGS GEORGE GERSHIN Vol.1
SR 60045*	Isn't It A Pity
MPL 6526 (E)	Of Thee I Sing
CMS 18011 (E)	I'll Build A Stairway To Paradise
MMC 14095 (E)	Someone To Watch Over Me
*Omitted	Bidin' My Time
	The Man I Love
	How Long Has This Been Going On
	My One And Only (What Am I Gonna Do)
	Lorelei
	I've Got A Crush On You
	Summertime*

MG 20311	SARAH VAUGHAN SINGS GEORGE GERSHWIN Vol.2
SR 60046	A Foggy Day
MPL 6527 (E)	Aren't You Kinda Glad We Did
CMS 18012 (E)	They All Laughed
MMC 14096 (E)	Looking For A Boy
	My Man's Gone Now
	He Loves And She Loves
	Do It Again
	Let's Call The Whole Thing Off
	Things Are Looking Up
	Love Walked In
	I Won't Say I Will

```
MG 20316                SARAH VAUGHAN AND BILLY ECKSTINE
SR 60002*               SING THE BEST OF IRVING BERLIN
MPL 6530 (E)            Alexander's Ragtime Band
CMS 18002* (E)          Isn't It A Lovely Day
MMC 14035 (E)           I've Got My Love To Keep Me Warm
*Omitted                Cheek To Cheek
CD Vogue                You're Just In Love
822526-2                Remember
                        Always
                        Now It Can Be Told*
                        Easter Parade

MG 20326                SARAH VAUGHAN AT MISTER KELLY'S
MPL 6542 (E)            September In The Rain
MVL 303 (E)             Willow Weep For Me
CD 832 791-2            Just One Of Those Things
plus 11 tracks          Be Anything But Darling Be Mine
                        Thou Swell
                        Stairway To The Stars
                        Honeysuckle Rose
                        Just A Gigolo
                        How High The Moon

MG 20370                VAUGHAN AND VIOLINS
SR 60038                Gone With The Wind
MPT 7518 (E)            Day By Day
CMS 18003 (E)           Please Be Kind
MMC 14011 (E)           Live For Love
                        I'll Close My Eyes
                        Misty
                        The Midnight Sun Will Never Set
                        That's All
                        I'm Lost
                        Love Me
                        The Thrill Is Gone

MG 20383                SARAH VAUGHAN AFTER HOURS
SR 60020                AT THE LONDON HOUSE
MMC 14001 (E)           Like Someone In Love
                        Detour Ahead
                        Three Little Words
                        I'll String Along With You
                        You'd Be So Nice To Come Home To
                        Speak Low
                        All Of You
                        Thanks For The Memory

MG 20438                THE MAGIC OF SARAH VAUGHAN
SR 60110                That Old Black Magic
                        Careless
                        Separate Ways
                        Are You Certain
                        Mary Contrary
                        Broken-Hearted Melody
                        I've Got The Word On A String
                        Don't Look At Me That Way
                        Love Is A Random Thing
                        Friendly Enemies
                        What's So Bad About It
```

Sweet Affection

MG 20441	NO COUNT SARAH
SR 60116	Smoke Gets In Your Eyes
MMC 14021 (E)	Doodlin'
CMS 18056 (E)	Darn That Dream
CD 824057-2	Just One Of Those Things
	Moonlight In Vermont
	No Count Blues
	Cheek To Cheek
	Stardust
	Missing You

MG 20493	14 NEWIES BUT GOODIES
SR 60172	Smooth Operator

MG 20511	GOLDEN GOODIES
SR 60217	Misty
	Broken-Hearted Melody

MG 20540	THE DIVINE SARAH VAUGHAN
SR 60255	I Still Believe In You
CD Vogue	Come Along With Me
600017	Imagination
	Hot And Cold Runnin' Tears
	That's Not The Kind Of Love I Want
	It's Love
	Leave It To Love
	You'll Find Me There
	Please Mr. Brown
	Gone Again
	The Next Time Around
	Padre

MG 20580	CLOSE TO YOU
SR 60240	Say It Isn't So
MMC 14059 (E)	Missing You
CMS 18040 (E)	I'll Never Be The Same
	There's No You
	I Should Care
	If You Are But A Dream
	Maybe You'll Be There
	Out Of This World
	Last Night When We Were Young
	Funny
	Close To You
	I've Got To Talk To My Heart

MG 20581	14 MORE NEWIES BUT GOODIES
SR 60241	You're My Baby

MG 20617	MY HEART SINGS
SR 60617	Never In A Million Years
20042 MCL (E)	My Ideal
20042 SMCL (E)	(All Of A Sudden) My Heart Sings
	Through A Long And Sleepless Night
	Please
	Slow Down
	The House I Live In

```
                        Our Waltz
                        Some Other Spring
                        Eternally
                        Maybe It's Because (I Love You Too Much)
                        Through The Years

MG 20645                SARAH VAUGHAN'S GOLDEN HITS
SR 60645                Misty
                        Broken-Hearted Melody
                        Make Yourself Comfortable
                        Autumn In New York
                        Moonlight In Vermont
                        How Important Can It Be
                        Smooth Operator
                        Whatever Lola Wants
                        Lullaby Of Birdland
                        Eternally
                        Poor Butterfly
                        Close To You

MG 20795                SPRING IS HERE
SR 60795                Easter Parade

MG 20813                IRVING BERLIN SONGS
SR 60813                Alexander's Ragtime Band
                        Always

MG 20831                SASSY SWINGS THE TIVOLI
SR 60831                Won't You Come Home Bill Bailey
20011 MCL (E)           Misty
20011 SMCL (E)          What Is This Thing Called Love
CD 832788-2             Lover man
plus 22 tracks          Sometimes I'm Happy
                        I Feel Pretty
                        Tenderly
                        Sassy's Blues
                        Polka Dots And Moonbeams
                        I Cried For You

MG 20882                VAUGHAN WITH VOICES
SR 60882                My Coloring Book
20014 MCL (E)           Hey There
20014 SMCL (E)          Deep Purple
6336 225 (E)            Days Of Wine And Roses
                        I'll Be Around
                        Funny
                        Charade
                        It Could Happen To You
                        This Heart Of Mine
                        Then I'll Be Tired Of You
                        How Beautiful Is Night
                        Blue Orchids

MG 20941                ! VIVA VAUGHAN !
SR 60941                The Boy From Ipanema
20046 MCL (E)           Fascinating Rhythm
2046 SMCL (E)           Night Song
6336 224 (E)            Mr. Lucky
                        Fever
```

                            Shiny Stockings
                            Avalon
                            Tea For Two
                            Quiet Nights (Corcovado)
                            Stompin' At The Savoy
                            Moment Of Truth
                            Jive Samba

MG 21009   MANCINI SONGBOOK
SR 61009   How Soon
20059 MCL (E)   The Days Of Wine And Roses
20059 SMCL (E)   Dear Heart
                            Charade
                            Too Little Time
                            Dreamsville
                            Bye-Bye (Theme From "Peter Gunn")
                            Moon River
                            (I Love You) And Don't You Forget It
                            Slow Hot Wind
                            Mr. Lucky
                            It Had Better Be Tonight

MG 21069   POP ARTISTRY
SR 61069   Yesterday
20085 MCL (E)*   I Know A Place
20085 SMCL (E)*   Little Hands*
*Omitted   Make It Easy On Yourself
(Night Song   He Touched Me
and Bye-Bye   Habibi
added)   What The World Needs Now Is Love
                            A Lover's Concerto
                            On A Clear Day You Can See Forever
                            First Thing Every Morning
                            Waltz For Debbie
                            If I Ruled The World*

MG 21079   NEW SCENE
SR 61079   One,Two,Three
20084 MCL (E)   What Now My Love
20084 SMCL (E)   Love
                            Who Can I Turn To
                            Call Me
                            With These Hands
                            Michelle
                            Sneakin' Up On You
                            Everybody Loves Somebody
                            The Shadow Of Your Smile
                            Dominique's Discotheque
                            I Should Have Kissed Him More

MG 21116   SASSY SWINGS AGAIN
SR 61116   Sweet Georgia Brown
20105 MCL (E)   Take The "A" Train
20105 SMCL (E)   I Left My Heart In San Francisco
CD 814 587-2   S'posin'
                            Everyday I Have The Blues
                            I Want To Be Happy
                            All Alone
                            The Sweetest Sounds

                          On The Other Side Of The Tracks
                          I Had A Ball

MG 21122   IT'S A MAN'S WORLD
SR 61122*   Alfie
21109 MCL (E)   Man That Got Away
21109 SMCL (E)   Trouble Is A Man
*Omitted   Happiness Is Just A Thing Called Joe
                          He's My Guy*
                          For Every Man There's A Woman
                          He's Funny That Way
                          My Man
                          I'm Just Wild About Harry
                          Show Me A Man I Can Look Up To*
                          Jim
                          Danny Boy

MG 25188   THE DIVINE SARAH
                          I Still Believe In You
                          My Funny Valentine
                          My One And Only Love
                          Come Along With Me
                          Imagination
                          It's Easy To Remember
                          And This Is My Beloved
                          Easy Come, Easy Go Lover

MG 25213   DIVINE SARAH SINGS
                          The Touch Of Your Lips
                          'S Wonderful
                          Tenderly
                          It's Magic
                          Honey
                          I'm In The Mood For Love
                          I Don't Know Why
                          Let's Put Out The Lights

MG 26005*   IMAGES
MPT 7518 (E)+   Shulie A Bop
*Omitted   Lover Man
+Omitted   Polka Dots And Moonbeams
                          Prelude To A Kiss
                          Pennies From Heaven*
                          If I Knew Then
                          Body And Soul
                          They Can't Take That Away From Me
                          You Hit The Spot+

MG 36004   SARAH VAUGHAN
20055 MCL (E)   Lullaby Of Birdland
MCL 125061 (E)   April In Paris
6336 329 (E)   He's My Guy
6336 709 (E)   Jim
                          You're Not The Kind
                          Embraceable You
                          I'm Glad There Is You
                          September Song
                          It's Crazy

MG 36058   SARAH VAUGHAN IN THE LAND OF HI-FI
EJL 100 (E)   Over The Rainbow
CD 826454-2   Soon
                  Cherokee
                  I'll Never Smile Again
                  Don't Be On The Outside
                  How High The Moon
                  It Shouldn't Happen To A Dream
                  Sometimes I'm Happy
                  Maybe
                  An Occasional Man
                  Why Can't I
                  Oh My

MG 36071   VOL.VIII THE JAZZ GIANTS
                  Shulie A Bop

MG 36086   FOR JAZZ LOVERS
                  It Shouldn't Happen To A Dream
                  Over The Rainbow

MG 36087   BARGAIN DAY !
                  Lullaby Of Birdland

MG 36088   UNDER ONE ROOF
                  Lush Life
                  I'm The Girl

MG 36089   SASSY
EJL 1258 (E)   Lush Life
                  Shake Down The Stars
                  I've Got Some Crying To Do
                  My Romance
                  I Loved Him
                  Lonely Woman
                  I'm Afraid The Masquerade Is Over
                  The Boy Next Door
                  Old Folks
                  Only You Can Say
                  A Sinner Kissed An Angel
                  I'm The Girl

MG 36109   SWINGIN' EASY
EJL 1273 (E)   Shulie A Bop
6336 713 (E)   Lover Man
CD 814641-2   I Cried For You
EJD-1025   Polka Dots And Moonbeams
                  All Of Me
                  Words Can't Describe
                  Prelude To A Kiss
                  You Hit The Spot
                  Pennies From Heaven
                  If I Knew Then
                  Body And Soul
                  They Can't That Away From Me

824 864-1   THE RODGERS AND HART SONGBOOK
CD 824 864-2   My Funny Valentine
                  Little Girl Blue

```
                    A Tree In The Park
                    It's Got To Be Love
                    A Ship Without A Sail
                    Bewitched
                    Thou Swell
                    It Never Entered My Mind
                    It's Easy To Remember
                    Why Can't I
                    My Romance
                    My Heart Stood Still

MGP2-100            SARAH VAUGHAN SINGS
                    GREAT SONGS FROM HIT SHOWS
                    As MG 20244 and 20245

MGP2-101            SARAH VAUGHAN SINGS GEORGE GERSHWIN
                    As MG 20310 and 20311

814 187-1           THE GEORGE GERSHWIN SONGBOOK
                    As MG 20318 and 20311

2 Em 412            LIVE
                    Intro:-September In The Rain
                    Just One Of Those Things
                    Be Anything But Darling Be Mine
                    Thou Swell
                    Stairway To The Stars
                    How High The Moon
                    Intro:-Like Someone In Love
                    Speak Low
                    Three Little Words
                    I'll String Along With You
                    All Of You
                    Thanks For The Memory
                    I Feel Pretty
                    Misty
                    What Is This Thing Called Love
                    Lover Man
                    Sometimes I'm Happy
                    Sassy's Blues
                    Polka Dots And Moonbeams
                    I Cried For You

SMCL 20155 (E)      PASSING STRANGERS
6463 041 (E)        As MG 20316 plus title song
6641 868 (E)
TIME 2 (E)

MPT 7506 (E)        POP PARADE Vol.2
                    The Other Woman

MPT 7523 (E)        POP PARADE Vol.4
                    Mr. Wonderful

MPT 7525 (E)        POP PARADE Vol.5
                    The Door Is Open
                    Poor Butterfly
```

SMWL 21017 (E)   LET'S PUT OUR SONG TOGETHER
                    As MG 20316

SMWL 21018 (E)   AFTER MIDNIGHT
                    Broken-Hearted Melody
                    Misty

SMWL 21054 (E)   MORE AFTER MIDNIGHT
                    Make Yourself Comfortable
                    Close To You

EJL 1250 (E)   TRIBUTE TO BROWNIE
                    You're Not The Kind

6619 035 (E)   SPOTLIGHT ON SARAH VAUGHAN
                    If This Isn't Love
                    Misty
                    All Alone
                    Who Can I Turn To
                    Bidin' My Time
                    Moonlight In Vermont
                    The Shadow Of Your Smile
                    Moon River
                    How Long Has This Been Going On
                    Soon
                    The Man I Love
                    Alfie
                    Let's Take An Old Fashioned Walk
                    Passing Strangers
                    Just One Of Those Things
                    Lost In The Stars
                    Call Me
                    Do It Again
                    How Soon
                    The Man That Got Away
                    A Tree In The Park
                    They Say It's Wonderful
                    He Loves And She Loves
                    What Now My love
                    All The Things You Are
                    A Ship Without A Sail
                    Happiness Is Just A Thing Called Joe
                    Cheek To Cheek

                    THE COMPLETE SARAH VAUGHAN ON MERCURY
                    Vol.1 GREAT JAZZ YEARS 1954-1959
18PJ-1030 (J)   I Still Believe In You
CD 836 320-2   My Funny Valentine
6 CDs   My One And Only Love
                    Come Along With Me
                    Imagination
                    It's Easy To Remember
                    And This Is My Beloved
                    Easy Come, Easy Go Lover
                    Lover Man
                    Shulie A Bop
                    Polka Dots And Moonbeams
                    Body And Soul
                    They Can't Take That Away From Me

Prelude To A Kiss
You Hit The Spot
If I Knew Then

18PJ-1031 (J)   Old Love
Old Devil Moon
Exactly Like You
Saturday
Idle Gossip
Make Yourself Comfortable
Oh Yeah
I'm In The Mood For Love
I Don't Know Why
Let's Put Out The Lights And Go To Sleep
Waltzing Down The Aisle
It's Magic
Honey
How Important Can It Be
The Touch Of Your Lips
'S Wonderful
Tenderly

18PJ-1032 (J)   September Song
Lullaby Of Birdland
Lullaby Of Birdland (edited master)
I'm Glad There Is You
You're Not The Kind
Jim
He's My Guy
April In Paris
It's Crazy
Embraceable You

18PJ-1033 (J)   Whatever Lola Wants
Slowly With Feeling
Experience Unnecessary
Fabulous Character
Johnny Be Smart
Hey, Naughty Papa
The Other Woman
Never
Never
C'est La Vie
C'est La Vie
Paradise
Time On My Hands
Time On My Hands
Gimme A Little Kiss
Mr. Wonderful
You Ought Have A Wife
Sometimes I'm Happy
Sometimes I'm Happy
Sometimes I'm Happy
Sometimes I'm Happy

18PJ-1034 (J)   I'll Never Smile Again
I'll Never Smile Again
I'll Never Smile Again
Don't Be On the Outside

Don't Be On The Outside
It Shouldn't Happen To A Dream
An Occasional Man
Soon
Cherokee
Maybe
Why Can't I
How High The Moon
Over The Rainbow
Over The Rainbow
Oh My
Oh My
Oh My

18PJ-1035 (J)   The Boy Next Door
Shake Down The Stars
I'm Afraid The Masquerade Is Over
Lush Life
A Sinner Kissed An Angel
Old Folks
The House I Live In
I'm The Girl
Hot And Cold Running Tears
The Edge Of The Sea
I've Got Some Crying To Do
That's Not The Kind Of Love I Want
My Romance
Lonely Woman
Only You Can Say
I Loved Him
It Happened Again
I Wanna Play House

                   Vol.2 SINGS GREAT AMERICAN SONGS 1956-1957
18PJ-1036 (J)   You're My Everything
CD 826 327-2   Autumn In New York
5 CDs   My Darling, My Darling
Little Girl Blue
Bewitched
Dancing In The Dark
Can't We Be Friends
All The Things You Are
It Never Entered My Mind
Homework
They Say It's Wonderful
The Touch Of Your Lips
My Heart Stood Still
Let's Take An Old Fashioned Walk
My Ship
A Tree In The Park
A Ship Without A Sail

18PJ-1037 (J)   He's Only Wonderful
But Not For Me
Poor Butterfly
Love Is A Random Thing
If I Loved You
September Song
Lost In The Stars

If This Isn't Love
It's Delovely
It's Love
Lucky In Love
It's Got To Be Love
Comes Love
The Bashful Matador
Leave It To Love
Don't Let Me Love You
The Second Time
April Gave Me One More Day
I've Got A New Heartache
Don't Look At Me That Way
The Banana Boat Song

18PJ-1038 (J)   Words Can't Describe
Pennies From Heaven
All Of Me
I Cried For You
Linger Awhile
Someone To Watch Over Me
A Foggy Day
Bidin' My Time
He Loves And She Loves
Love Walked In
Looking For A Boy
I've Got A Crush On You
Isn't It A Pity
Do It Again
How Long Has This Been Going On
Aren't You Kinda Glad We Did
The Man I Love

18PJ-1039   Let's Call The Whole Thing Off
They All Laughed
Lorelei
I'll Build A Stairway To Paradise
Summertime
Things Are Looking Up
I Won't Say I Will
Of Thee I Sing
Of Thee I Sing
My One And Only Love
Isn't It A Lovely Day
Easter Parade
Now It Can Be Told

18PJ-1040   Alexander's Ragtime Band
I've Got My Love To Keep Me Warm
You're Just In Love
My Man's Gone Now
Cheek To Cheek
Remember
Always
Passing Strangers
The Door Is Open
You'll Find Me There
Please Mr.Brown
Please Mr.Brown

                        Band Of Angels
                        Slow Down
                        Goodnight Kiss
                        No Limit

                        Vol.3 GREAT SHOW ON STAGE 1957-1959
18PJ-1041 (J)   September In The Rain
CD 826 333-2   Willow Weep for Me
6 CDs   Just One Of Those Things
                        Be Anything But Darling Be Mine
                        Thou Swell
                        Stairway To The Stars
                        Honeysuckle Rose
                        Just A Gigolo
                        How High The Moon
                        Dream
                        I'm Gonna Sit Right Down And Write Myself
                          A Letter
                        It's Got To Be Love
                        Alone
                        It's Got To Be Love

18PJ-1042 (J)   If This Isn't Love
                        Embraceable You
                        Lucky In Love
                        Dancing In The Dark
                        Poor Butterfly
                        Sometimes I'm Happy
                        I Cover The Waterfront
                        Sweet Affection
                        Meet Me Halfway
                        What's So Bad About It
                        That Old Black Magic
                        That Old Black Magic
                        I've Got The World On A String
                        I've Got The World On A String
                        Hit The Road To Dreamland

18PJ-1043 (J)   Gone Again
                        The Next Time Around
                        Careless
                        Friendly Enemies
                        Are You Certain
                        Stardust
                        Doodlin'
                        Doodlin'
                        Darn That Dream
                        Darn That Dream
                        Darn That Dream
                        Mary Contrary
                        Separate Ways
                        Broken-Hearted Melody
                        Too Much Too Soon
                        Padre
                        Spin Little Bottle

18PJ-1044 (J)   Smoke Gets In Your Eyes
                        Moonlight In Vermont
                        Cheek To Cheek

```
                    Missing You
                    Just One Of Those Things
                    No Count Sarah
                    Detour Ahead
                    Three Little Words
                    Speak Low
                    Like Someone In Love
                    You'd Be So Nice To Come Home To
                    I'll String Along With You
                    All Of You
                    Thanks For The Memory

18PJ-1045 (J)       Please Be Kind
                    The Midnight Sun Will Never Set
                    Live For Love
                    Misty
                    I'm Lost
                    Love Me
                    That's All
                    Day By Day
                    Gone With The Wind
                    I'll Close My Eyes
                    The Thrill Is Gone
                    Cool Baby
                    Everything I Do
                    I Ain't Hurtin'
                    Disillusioned Heart
                    I Should Care
                    For All We Know

18PJ-1046 (J)       My Ideal
                    You're My Baby
                    Smooth Operator
                    Maybe It's Because I Love You Too Much
                    Our Waltz
                    Never In A Million Years
                    Close To You
                    Eternally
                    Some Other Spring
                    Say It Isn't So
                    If You Are But A Dream
                    Maybe You'll Be There
                    (All Of A Sudden) My Heart Sings
                    There's No You
                    Missing You
                    Please
                    Funny
                    I've Got To Talk To My Heart
                    Out Of This World
                    Last Night When We Were Young
                    Through A Long And Sleepless Night
                    I'll Never Be The Same
                    Through The Years

                    Vol.4 (part 1) LIVE IN EUROPE 1963-1964
18PJ-1074 (J)       He Never Mentioned Love
CD 830 714-2        Gone
6 CDs               Right Or Wrong
                    Show Me A Man
```

```
                       I Feel Pretty
                       Misty
                       What Is This Thing Called Love
                       Lover Man
                       Sometimes I'm Happy
                       Won't You Come Home Bill Bailey
                       Tenderly
                       Sassy's Blues
                       Polka Dots And Moonbeams
                       I Cried For You

18PJ-1075 (J)          Poor Butterfly
                       I Could Write A Book
                       Time After Time
                       All Of Me
                       I Hadn't Anyone 'Till You
                       I Can't Give You Anything But Love
                       I'll Be Seeing You
                       Maria
                       Day In,  Day Out
                       Fly Me To The Moon
                       Baubles, Bangles And Beads
                       The Lady's In Love With You

18PJ-1076 (J)          Honeysuckle Rose
                       What Is This Thing Called Love
                       Lover Man
                       I Cried For You
                       The More I See You
                       Say It Isn't So
                       Black Coffee
                       Just One Of Those Things
                       On Green Dolphin Street
                       Over The Rainbow

18PJ-1077 (J)          Charade
                       It Could Happen To You
                       Blue Orchids
                       This Heart Of Mine
                       Then I'll Be Tired Of You
                       Funny
                       My Coloring Book
                       How Beautiful Is Night
                       Hey There
                       Deep Purple
                       I'll Be Around
                       Days Of Wine And Roses

                       Vol.4 (part 2) SASSY SWINGS AGAIN 1964-1967
18PJ-1078 (J)          How's The World Treating You
                       My Darling, My Darling
                       Bluesette
                       You Got It Made
                       Make Someone Happy
                       Sole, Sole
                       Mr.Lucky
                       The Boy From Ipenema
                       Quiet Nights (Corcovado)
                       Jive Samba
```

A Taste Of Honey
Shiny Stockings
Night Song
Stomping At The Savoy
Fascinating Rhythm
The Moment Of Truth
Tea For Two
Fever
Avalon

18PJ-1079 (J)   We Almost Made It
How Soon
Dear Heart
Too Little Time
Dreamsville
Bye-Bye (Theme From "Peter Gunn")
Moon River
(I Love You and) Don't You Forget It
Slow Hot Wind
It Had Better Be Tonight
Pawnbroker's Theme
Darling
I'll Never Be Lonely Again
Habibi

18PJ-1080 (J)   Make It Easy On Yourself
What The World Needs Now Is Love
I Know A Place
Little Hands
Yesterday
A Lover's Concerto
He Touched Me
If I Ruled The World
Waltz For Debbie
On A Clear Day You Can See Forever
The First Thing Every Morning
Who Can I Turn To
The Shadow Of Your Smile
I Should Have Kissed Him More
Call Me
With These Hands
Dominique's Discotheque
Everybody Loves Somebody

18PJ-1081 (J)   What Now My Love
Love
One, Two, Three
Michelle
Sneakin' Up On You
Jim
Man That Got Away
My Man
Happiness Is Just A Thing Called Joe
Trouble Is A Man
He's Funny That Way
For Every Man There's A Woman
I'm Just Wild About Harry
Danny Boy
Alfie

18PJ-1082 (J)   On The Other Side Of The Tracks
                     All Alone
                     I Want To Be Happy
                     S'posin'
                     I Had A Ball
                     Take The "A" Train
                     I Left My Heart In San Francisco
                     The Sweetest Sounds
                     Everyday I Have The Blues
                     Sweet Georgia Brown

MUSICRAFT

MVS 504   DIVINE SARAH
                     If You Could See Me Now
                     I Can Make You Love Me
                     You're Not The Kind
                     My Kinda Love
                     I've Got A Crush On You
                     I'm Thru With Love
                     Everything I Have Is Yours
                     Body And Soul
                     I Cover The Waterfront
                     Ghost Of A Chance
                     Tenderly
                     Don't Blame Me
                     The Lord's Prayer
                     Sometimes I Feel Like A Motherless Child

MVS 509   GEORGIE AULD AND HIS ORCHESTRA Vol.2
                     You're Blase
                     A Hundred Years From Today

MVS 2001   TEDDY WILSON WITH SARAH VAUGHAN
                     September Song
                     When We're Alone
                     Time After Time
                     Don't Worry 'Bout Me

MVS 2002   SARAH VAUGHAN Vol.2
                     Trouble Is A Man
                     I'm Gonna Sit Right Down And Write Myself
                       A Letter
                     I Can't Get Started
                     The Man I Love
                     The One I Love Belongs To Somebody Else
                     It's You Or No-One
                     Once In A While
                     I Get A Kick Out Of You
                     I'll Wait And Pray
                     I'm Glad There Is You
                     Time And Again
CDs of above LPs are included on It's You Or No-One MVSCD-55:
Tenderly MVSCD-57: Time And Again MVSCD-61: plus early tracks

PABLO DE LUXE

2310 821   HOW LONG HAS THIS BEEN GOING ON
                     I've Got The World On A String

```
CD                    Midnight Sun
PACD 2310 821-2       How Long Has This Been Going On
                      You're Blase
                      Easy Livin'
                      More Than You Know
                      My Old Flame
                      Teach Me Tonight
                      Body And Soul
                      When Your Lover Has Gone

2310 823              MILT JACKSON + COUNT BASIE + THE BIG BAND
                      Vol.2
                      Lena And Lennie

2312 101              I LOVE BRAZIL
110 0018 (Br)*        If You Went Away
*Omitted              Triste
Someone To            Roses And Roses
Light Up My           Vera Cruz*
Life and              I Live To Love You
Bridges added         The Face I Love
                      Courage
                      The Day It Rained
                      A Little Tear*
                      Cantador*

2312 111              DUKE ELLINGTON SONGBOOK ONE
CD                    In A Sentimental Mood
PACD 2312 111-2       I'm  Just A Lucky So And So
                      Solitude
                      I Let A Song Go Out Of My Heart
                      I Didn't Know About You
                      All Too Soon
                      Lush Life
                      In A Mellow Tone
                      Sophisticated Lady
                      Day Dream

2312 116              DUKE ELLINGTON SONGBOOK TWO
CD                    I Ain't Got Nothing But The Blues
PACD 2312 116-2       Black Butterfly
                      Chelsea Bridge
                      What Am I Here For
                      Tonight I Shall Sleep
                      Rocks In My Bed
                      I Got It Bad And That Ain't Good
                      Everything But You
                      Mood Indigo
                      It Don't Mean A Thing
                      Prelude To A Kiss

2312 119              CELEBRATION OF DUKE
                      I Ain't Got Nothing But The Blues
                      Everything But You

2312 125              COPACABANA
                      Copacabana
                      The Smiling Hour
                      To Say Goodbye
```

```
                        Dreamer
                        Gentle Rain
                        Tete
                        Dindi
                        Double Rainbow
                        Bonita

2312 130                SEND IN THE CLOWNS
                        I Got A Right To Sing The Blues
                        Just Friends
                        Ill Wind
                        If You Could See Me Now
                        I Hadn't Anyone 'Till You
                        Send In The Clowns
                        All The Things You Are
                        Indian Summer
                        When Your Lover Has Gone
                        From This Moment On

2312 137                CRAZY AND MIXED UP
CD                      I Didn't Know What Time It Was
PACD 2312 137-2         That's All
                        Autumn Leaves
                        Love Dance
                        The Island
                        In Love In Vain
                        Seasons
                        You Are Too Beautiful

2312 885                BEST OF SARAH VAUGHAN
                        You're Blase
                        I've Got The World On A String
                        The Midnight Sun
                        I've Got A Right To Sing The Blues
                        From This Moment On
                        Ill Wind
                        All Too Soon
                        Lush Life
                        In A Sentimental Mood
                        Dindi

PRONIT (P)

SX 0605 (P)             JAZZ JAMBOREE '75
                        The Man I Love
                        I Got It Bad And That Ain't Good
                        On A Clear Day You Can See Forever
                        Misty
                        A Foggy Day
                        'Round Midnight
                        Close To You
                        What Are You Doing The Rest Of Your Life
                        Sassy's Blues
                        The Nearness Of You
                        Just A Gigolo
                        My Funny Valentine
                        Bill Bailey Won't You Please Come Home
```

PYE (E)

NSPL 18544 (E)   RONNIE SCOTT PRESENTS SARAH VAUGHAN
                      Here's That Rainy Day
                      Like Someone In Love
                      Feelings
                      I'll Remember April
                      Sophisticated Lady
                      If You Could See Me Now
                      Start Believing In Me
                      My Funny Valentine
                      A Foggy Day
                      Send In The Clowns
                      Tenderly

N 103 (E)   RONNIE SCOTT PRESENTS SARAH VAUGHAN Vol.2
                      The Man I Love
                      Passing Strangers
                      Gershwin Medley;- But Not For Me
                                         Our Love Is Here To Stay
                                         Someone To Watch Over Me
                      Blue Skies
                      The More I See You
                      Early Autumn
                      On A Clear Day You Can See Forever
                      Everything Must Change
                      I Cried For You

5008 (E)   RONNIE SCOTT'S 20th ANNIVERSARY ALBUM
                      Here's That Rainy Day

Q-WEST

926020-1   BACK ON THE BLOCK
(E) WEA 9260202   Jazz Corner Of The Word
CD 926020-2   Birdland
                      Septembro (Brazilian Wedding Song)
                      Wee B. Dooinit (A Capella Party)

ROULETTE/COLUMBIA (E)

42109   YOU'RE MINE YOU
                      You're Mine You
                      The Best Is Yet To Come
                      Witchcraft
                      So Long
                      The Second Time Around
                      I Could Write A Book
                      Maria
                      Baubles, Bangles And Beads
                      Fly Me To The Moon
                      Moonglow
                      Invitation
                      On Green Dolphin Street

52046   DREAMY
33SX 1252 (E)   Dreamy
SCX 3324 (E)   Hands Across The Table
                      The More I See You

                            I'll Be Seeing You
                            Star Eyes
                            You've Changed
                            Trees
                            Why Was I Born
                            My Ideal
                            Crazy He Calls Me
                            Stormy Weather
                            Moon Over Miami

52050   THE MOST Vol.1
                            You've Changed
                            Why Was I Born

52053   THE MOST Vol.2
                            Moon Over Miami
                            Trees

52057   THE MOST Vol.3
                            Crazy He Calls Me
                            Stormy Weather

52060   DIVINE ONE
33SX 1340 (E)   Have You Met Miss Jones
SCX 3390 (E)   Ain't No Use
                            Everytime I See You
                            You Stepped Out Of A Dream
                            Gloomy Sunday
                            What Do You See In Her
                            Jump For Joy
                            When Your Lover Has Gone
                            I'm Gonna Laugh You Right Out Of My Life
                            Wrap Your Trouble In Dreams
                            Someone Else's Dream
                            Trouble Is A Man

52061   COUNT BASIE-SARAH VAUGHAN
33SX 1360 (E)   Perdido
SCX 3403 (E)   Lover Man
CD   I Cried For You
RCD 59043   Alone
                            There Are Such Things
                            Mean To Me
                            The Gentleman Is A Dope
                            You Go To My Head
                            Until There Was You
                            You Turned The Tables On Me
                            Little Man You've Had A Busy Day

52062   THE MOST Vol.4
                            Serenata

52070   AFTER HOURS
33SX 1405 (E)   My Favorite Things
CD Vogue   Ev'ry Time We Say Goodbye
600182 includes   Wonder Why
Plus 2 below   Easy To Love
                            Sophisticated Lady
                            Great Day

```
                         Ill Wind
                         If Love Is Good To me
                         In A Sentimental Mood
                         Vanity

52075                    THE MOST Vol.5
                         Little Man You've Had A Busy Day
                         Have You Met Miss Jones

52082                    YOU'RE MINE YOU
33SX 1438 (E)            Stereo Version Of 42019
SCX 3444 (E)

52091                    SNOWBOUND
33SX 1542 (E)            Snowbound
SCX 3489 (E)             I Hadn't Anyone 'Till You
                         What's Good About Goodbye
                         Stella By Starlight
                         Look To Your Heart
                         Oh, You Crazy Moon
                         Blah, Blah, Blah
                         I Remember You
                         I Fall In Love Too Easily
                         Glad To Be Unhappy
                         Spring Can Really Hang You Up The Most

52092                    THE EXPLOSIVE SIDE OF SARAH VAUGHAN
33SX 1523 (E)            I Believe In You
SCX 3479 (E)             Honeysuckle Rose
RSD-308 (E)              Moonlight On The Ganges
                         The Lady's In Love With You
                         After You've Gone
                         Garden In The Rain
                         I Can't Give You Anything But Love
                         The Trolley Song
                         I'm Gonna Live 'Till I Die
                         Falling In Love With Love
                         Great Day
                         Nobody Else But Me

52100                    STAR EYES
33SX 1592 (E)            Star Eyes
SCX 3507 (E)             Once Upon A Summertime
                         Don't Go To Strangers
                         Icy Stone
                         I Was Telling Him About You
                         I'll Never Be The Same
                         Call Me Irresponsible
                         Bewildered
                         Do You Remember
                         There'll Be Other Times
                         Within Me I Know
                         As Long As He Needs Me

52104                    LONELY HOURS
33SX 1651 (E)            Lonely Hours
                         I'll Never Be The Same
                         If I Had You
                         Friendless
```

You're Driving Me Crazy
Always On My Mind
Look For Me I'll Be Around
What'll I Do
Solitude
These Foolish Things
The Man I Love
So Long My Love

52108   WE THREE
33SX 1645   Fly Me To The Moon
               I Can't Give You Anything But Love
               Only
               Serenata

52109   THE WORLD OF SARAH VAUGHAN
               Fly Me To The Moon
               Key Largo
               Wallflower Waltz
               Jump For Joy
               My Dear Little Sweetheart
               Moonlight On The Ganges
               Marie
               My Favorite Things
               Mama, He Treats Your Daughter Mean
               Stella By Starlight
               The Gravy Waltz
               Call Me Irresponsible

52112   SWEET N' SASSY
33SX 1697 (E) I Didn't Know About You
               More Than You Know
               Thanks For The Ride
               Comes Spring
               I Wish I Were In Love Again
               A Lazy Afternoon
               Just Married Today
               Something I Dreamed Last Night
               I Got Rhythm
               This Can't Be Love
               Slowly
               Just You, Just Me

52111   COUNT BASIE-COMMAND PERFORMANCE
               Mean To Me
               Until I Met You

52116   SINGS SOULFULLY
33SX 1726 (E) A Taste Of Honey
SCX 3553 (E)   What Kind Of Fool Am I
               I Guess I'll Hang My Tears Out To Dry
               Sermonette
               In Love In Vain
               The Gravy Waltz
               The Good Life
               'Round Midnight
               Easy Street
               Baby Won't You Please Come Home
               The Midnight Sun

```
52118              PLUS TWO
CD Vogue           Just In Time
600182 plus        When Sunny Gets Blue
After Hours LP     All I Do Is Dream Of You
                   I Understand
                   Goodnight Sweetheart
                   Baby Won't You Please Come Home
                   When Lights Are Low
                   Key Largo
                   Just Squeeze Me
                   All Or Nothing At All
                   The Very Thought Of you

52123              SLIGHTLY CLASSICAL
CD                 Be My Love
CDP 7959772        Intermezzo
(E)CD-Rou 1029     I Give To You
plus 5 titles      Because
                   Full Moon And Empty Arms
                   My Reverie
                   Moonlight Love
                   Ah, Sweet Mystery Of Life

RE 105             THE SARAH VAUGHAN YEARS
                   Call Me Irresponsible
                   Mama
                   Just Married Today
                   My Ideal
                   Ain't No Use
                   I'll Be Seeing You
                   Little Man You've Had A Busy Day
                   I Wish I Were In Love Again
                   I Remember You
                   Slowly
                   You're Mine You
                   The Lady's In Love With You
                   Only
                   Lonely Hours
                   Lazy Afternoon
                   This Can't Be Love
                   I Was Telling Him About You
                   The Wallflower Waltz
                   Nobody Else But You
                   Something I Dreamed Last Night

RE 107             THE COUNT BASIE YEARS
                   You've Changed
                   You Go To My Head
                   The Gentleman Is A Dope
                   Lover Man
                   Mean To Me

RE 127             BIRDLAND ALLSTARS LIVE AT CARNEGIE HALL
                   Perdido
                   Polka Dots And Moonbeams
                   Medley;- I Ain't Mad At You
                             Summertime
                   Saturday
                   Time
```

That Old Devil Moon
Tenderly
Don't Blame Me

RE 103 (E)   THE SARAH VAUGHAN YEARS
Perdido
The Second Time Around
Comes Spring
The Man I Love
My Ideal
Witchcraft
When Sunny Gets Blue
Slowly
As Long As She Needs Me
The Lady's In Love With You
Moonglow
You've Changed
These Foolish Things
Gloomy Sunday
When You're Lover Has Gone
Icy Stone
Stella By Starlight
The Midnight Sun
I'll Be Seeing You

2682 031 (E)   THE SUMMIT MEETING
Perdido
Lover Man
I Cried For You
There Are Such Things
Mean To Me
The Gentleman Is A Dope
Until I Met You
You Turned The Tables On Me

2682 032 (E)   THE INTIMATE
Have You Met Miss Jones
My Favorite Things
Ev'ry Time We Say Goodbye
Wonder Why
Easy To Love
Sophisticated Lady
Ain't No Use
You Stepped Out Of A Dream
Great Day
Ill Wind
If Love Is Good To Me
In A Sentimental Mood
Vanity
Gloomy Sunday
Jump For Joy
When Sunny Gets Blue
All I Do Is Dream Of You
I Understand
Goodnight Sweetheart
When Your Lover Has Gone
Wrap Your Troubles In Dreams
Baby, Won't You Please Come Home
When Lights Are Low

Key Largo
Just Squeeze Me
All Or Nothing At All
The Very Thought Of You

2682 043 (E)   ON THE SWINGIN' SIDE
                    Baubles, Bangles And Beads
                    The Best Is Yet To Come
                    Witchcraft
                    So Long
                    I Could Write A Book
                    On Green Dolphin Street
                    Moonglow
                    After You've Gone
                    The Trolley Song
                    A Taste Of Honey
                    Sermonette
                    The Good Life
                    Easy Street
                    I Believe In You
                    The Gravy Waltz
                    I Can't Give You Anything But Love
                    Great Day
                    Honeysuckle Rose
                    Moanin'
                    'Round Midnight
                    Moonlight On The Ganges
                    The Lady's In Love With You
                    The Midnight Sun
                    A Garden In The Rain
                    I'm Gonna Live 'Till I Die
                    Falling In Love With Love
                    I Wish I Were In Love Again
                    Nobody Else But Me
                    Just You, Just Me
                    Baby Won't You Please Come Home
                    This Can't Be Love
                    I Got Rhythm

ROU 1020 (E)   THE SARAH VAUGHAN YEARS Vol.1
CD Rou 1020   Ev'ry Time We Say Goodbye
including   Great Day
Vol 2   Just In Time
                    You Stepped Out Of A Dream
                    Have You Met Miss Jones
                    Jump For Joy
                    Perdido
                    I Cried For You
                    Mean To Me
                    Lover Man
                    Honeysuckle Rose
                    I Can't Give You Anything But Love

ROU 1021 (E)   THE SARAH VAUGHAN YEARS Vol.2
                    When Lights Are Low
                    All Or Nothing At All
                    'Round Midnight
                    Solitude
                    I'll Never Be The Same

                    The Man I Love
                    I'll Be Seeing You
                    Maria
                    I Fall In Love Too Easily
                    Glad To Be Unhappy
                    Spring Can Really Hang You Up The Most
                    I Remember You

ROU 1022 (E)   THE SINGLES SESSIONS
CD Rou 1022   Serenata
                    My Dear Little Sweetheart
                    The Green Leaves Of Summer
                    Them There Eyes
                    Don't Go To Strangers
                    Love
                    What's The Use
                    Wallflower Waltz
                    True Believer
                    April
                    If Not For You
                    Oh, Lover
                    One Mint Julep
                    Mama, He Treats Your Daughter Mean

ARTIA PARLIAMENT

WMGS 2   THE WORLD'S GREATEST MUSIC-JAZZ
                    Teach Me Tonight
                    In Other Words
                    You Turned The Tables On Me
                    Trees
                    Hands Across The Table
                    Ain't No Use
                    In A Sentimental Mood
                    The Best Is Yet To Come
                    Maria
                    Ev'ry Time We Say Goodbye
                    You Stepped Out Of A Dream
                    When Your Lover Has Gone
                    Why Was I Born

WPOM 6   title not known
                    You Turned The Tables On Me

SESSION DISC

SR 124   APOLLO HALL
                   Street Of Dreams

WARNER

BSK 3653   SHARKY'S MACHINE Soundtrack
104105 (E)   Love Theme
                   Before You

Singles And EPs

ALLADIN

3019   We're Through

BELL

B 832   A Time For Love Is Anytime

BRAVO (E)

BR 305 (E)   SARAH VAUGHAN
                    What A Diff'rence A Day Made
                    A Hundred Years From Today
                    Lover Man
                    My Kinda Love

BRR 381 (E)   WITH THE QUINCY JONES ORCHESTRA
                    Moonglow
                    So Long
                    Maria
                    Invitation

COLUMBIA

38461   Bianca

38462   As You Desire Me
                    Black Coffee
38512   While You're Gone
                    Tonight I Shall Sleep
38551   Give Me A Song With A Beautiful Melody

38559   That Lucky Old Sun
                    Make Believe
38617   Fool's Paradise
                    Lonely Girl
38630   You Say You Care
                    I Cried For You

38701	I'm Crazy To Love You
	Summertime
38810	You Taught Me To Love Again
	Just Friends
38860	Our Very Own
	Don't Be Afraid
38896	Ain't Misbehavin'
	East Of The Sun
38897	Goodnight My Love
	Nice Work If You Can Get It
38898	Can't Get Out Of This Mood
	Come Rain Or Come Shine
38899	It Might As Well Be Spring
	Mean To Me
38925	I Love The Guy
	Thinking Of You
39001	Perdido
	Whippa, Whippa, Will
39071	You're Mine You
	The Nearness Of You
39124	I'll Know
	De Gas Pipe She Is Leakin' Joe
39207	Ave Maria
	A City Called Heaven
39370	Deep Purple
	These Things I Offer You
39446	Vanity
	My Reverie
39494	Out Of Breath
	After Hours
39576	Just A Moment More
	I Ran All The Way Home
39634	Pinky
	A Miracle Happened
39719	Corner To Corner
	If Someone Had Told Me
39789	Street Of Dreams
	Time To Go
39839	Say You'll Wait For Me
	My Tormented Heart
39873	Sinner Or Saint
	Mighty Lonesome Feeling
39932	I Confess
	Lover's Quarrel
39963	Spring Will Be A Little Late This Year
	A Blues Serenade
40041	Time
	Linger Awhile
50046	You're Mine You
	The Nearness Of You
50072	As You Desire Me
	Black Coffee
52142	I Cried For You
	Summertime
52143	You're Mine You
	After Hours
B 1631	DEEP PURPLE
	Deep Purple

```
                    Just Friends
                    Street Of Dreams
                    You Taught Me To Love Again

B 2551              title not known
                    Deep Purple
                    You're Mine You
                    Street Of Dreams
                    The Nearness Of You

B 2588              SARAH VAUGHAN
                    Perdido
                    Linger Awhile
                    Time
                    Corner To Corner

B 7451              SARAH VAUGHAN IN HI-FI
                    East Of The Sun
                    Nice Work If You Can Get It
                    Pinky
                    The Nearness Of You

B 7452              SARAH VAUGHAN IN HI-FI
                    Come Rain Or Come Shine
                    Mean To Me
                    It Might As Well Be Spring
                    Can't Get Out Of This Mood

B 7453              SARAH VAUGHAN IN HI-FI
                    Spring Will Be A Little Late This Year
                    Ooh What-cha Doin' To Me
                    Goodnight My Love
                    Ain't Misbehavin'

B 9141              LINGER AWHILE
                    Linger Awhile
                    These Things I Offer You
                    A Lover's Quarrel
                    I Confess

B 9142              LINGER AWHILE
                    Just A Moment More
                    Sinner Or Saint
                    My Tormented Heart

B 9143              LINGER AWHILE
                    Don't Be Afraid
                    I'm Crazy To Love You
                    Mighty Lonesome Feeling
                    A Blues Serenade

B 324               POPULAR FAVORITES Vol VI
                    My Tormented Heart

B 777               S64,000 JAZZ
                    Perdido

B 211               SARAH SINGS
(Double EP)         East Of The Sun
```

```
C 211              Ain't Misbehavin'
(78 Set)           Goodnight My Love
                   Nice Work If You Can Get It
                   Come Rain Or Come Shine
                   Can't Get Out Of This Mood
                   Mean To Me
                   It Might As Well Be Spring

B 490              AFTER HOURS
(Double EP)        After Hours
                   Summertime
                   You're Mine You
                   My Reverie
                   Black Coffee
                   Thinking Of You
                   I Cried For You
                   Perdido
```

COLUMBIA (E)

```
DB 2600 (E)        That Lucky Old Sun
                   As You Desire Me
DB 2771 (E)        Thinking Of You
                   ----------------
DB 3172 (E)        My Tormented Heart
                   Say You'll Wait For Me
DB 3197 (E)        Sinner Or Saint
                   Mighty Lonesome Feeling
DB 4491 (E)        My Dear Little Sweetheart
                   Ooh, What A Day
DB 4511 (E)        If I Were A Bell
                   Teach Me Tonight
DB 4542 (E)        Serenata
                   Let's
DB 4634 (E)        What's The Use
                   True Believer
DB 4807 (E)        One Mint Julep
                   Mama
DB 4901 (E)        Moonglow
                   The Second Time Around
DB 4990 (E)        My Favorite Things
                   Great Day
DB 7378 (E)        A Garden In The Rain
                   I Can't Give You Anything But Love
DB 7500 (E)        I Got Rhythm
                   I Wish I Were In Love Again
```

CONTINENTAL

```
6008               What More Can A Woman Do
                   I'd Rather Have A Memory Than A Dream
6024               Mean To Me
                   Signing Off
6031               Interlude
                   East Of The Sun
6061               No Smokes
                   ---------
```

CROWN

107	I'm Scared
108	It Might As Well Be Spring
109	You Go To My Head
118	I Could Make You Love Me

DE LUXE

2003	I'll Wait And Pray
3003	I'll Wait And Pray

EMBER (E)

EMB 4523 (E)   DIVINE SARAH VAUGHAN
September Song
Don't Worry 'Bout Me
Lover Man
I Feel So Smoochie

GOTHAM

105   All Too Soon

GUILD

1002   Lover Man

HRS

HRS 1019   We're Through

LONDON (E)

HBU 1049   SARAH VAUGHAN SINGS
It Might As Well Be Spring
I Can Make You Love Me
You Go To My Head
I'm Scared

MAINSTREAM

5512	Imagine
	Sweet Gingerbread Man
5517	Inner City Blues
	On Thinking It Over
5521	Pieces Of Dreams
	Once You've Been In Love
5522	The Summer Knows
	What Are You Doing The Rest Of Your Life

5523	The Story Of Frasier
	Summer Me, Winter Me
5527	And The Feelings Good
	Deep In The Night
5533	Just A Little Lovin'
	Rainy Days And Mondays
5541	Send In The Clowns

5544	Alone Again (Naturally)
	Run To Me
5553	Do Away With April
	I Need You More

MERCURY/EMARCY

70086	It Shouldn't Happen To A Dream
	Over The Rainbow
70299	And This Is My Beloved
	Easy Come, Easy Go Lover
70331	Come Along With Me
	It's Easy To Remember
70423	Old Devil Moon
	Saturday
70469	Idle Gossip
	Make Yourself Comfortable
70534	Waltzing Down The Aisle
	How Important Can It Be
70595	Oh Yeah
	Whatever Lola Wants
70646	Experiance Unnecessary
	Slowly With Feeling
70693	Johnny Be Smart
	Hey Naughty Papa
70727	Never
	C'est La Vie
70777	Mr. Wonderful
	You Ought Have A Wife
70846	Hot And Cold Running Tears
	That's Not The Kind Of Love
70885	Fabulous Character
	The Other Woman
70947	It Happened Again
	I Wanna Play House
71020	I've Got A New Heartache
	The Banana Boat Song
71030	The Bashful Matador
	Leave It To Love
71085	April Gave Me One More Day
	Poor Butterfly
71122	Passing Strangers
	The Door Is Open
71157	Please Mr. Brown
	Band Of Angels
71235	Gone Again
	Next Time Around
71303	Spin Little Bottle
	Padre
71326	Too Much, Too Soon
	What's So Bad About It

71380	Everything I Do
	I Ain't Hurtin'
71393	No Limit
	Alexander's Ragtime Band
71407	Cool Baby
	Are You Certain
71433	Careless
	Separate Ways
71477	Broken-Hearted Melody
	Misty
71519	Maybe It's Because
	Smooth Operator
71562	You're My Baby
	Eternally
71610	Our Waltz
	Some Other Spring
71642	Maybe You'll Be There
	Doodlin'
71669	For All We Know
	Through The Years
71702	Close To You
	Out Of This World
71742	If You Are But A Dream
	Mary Contrary
72187	Gone
	Show Me A Man
72249	Bluesette
	You Got It Made
72300	How's The World Treating You
	Sole, Sole
72334	Mr. Lucky
	Fever
72381	We Almost Made It
	The Other Half Of Me
73417	Pawnbroker's Theme
	Peter Gunn
72510	Darling
	I'll Never Be Lonely Again
72543	First Thing Every Morning
	A Lover's Concerto
30031	Lullaby Of Birdland
	Poor Butterfly
30092	Misty
	Broken-Hearted Melody
16005	Polka Dots And Moonbeams
	Shulie A Bop
3232	SARAH VAUGHAN SINGS
	Easy Come, Easy Go Lover
	It's Easy To Remember
	My Funny Valentine
	Imagination
3287	SARAH VAUGHAN
	Old Devil Moon
	Make Yourself Comfortable
	Idle Gossip
	Saturday

3304   DIVINE SARAH SINGS
                It's Magic
                'S Wonderful
                Tenderly
                The Touch Of Your Lips

3305   SONGS BY SARAH
                Honey
                I'm In The Mood For Love
                Let's Put Out The Lights And Go To Sleep
                I Don't Know Why

3324   DAMNED YANKEES
                Whatever Lola Wants

3396   DIVINE SARAH
                Smooth Operator
                You're My Baby
                Eternally
                Broken-Hearted Melody

3507   SARAH VAUGHAN
                The Bashful Matador
                Leave It To Love
                The Banana Boat Song
                I've Got A New Heartache

4017   TOPS IN POPS Vol.1
                Whatever Lola Wants
                How Important Can It Be
                Waltzing Down The Aisle
                Oh Yeah

4018   TOPS IN POPS Vol.2
                Johnny Be Smart

4019   TOPS IN POPS Vol.3
                C'est La Vie

4021   TOPS IN POPS Vol.5
                Mr. Wonderful

4026   TOPS IN POPS Vol.10
                Fabulous Character


```
4042              VAUGHAN AND VIOLINS
                  Please Be Kind
                  Misty
                  Day By Day
                  Gone With The Wind

SNP 133           THE COMPLETE STARDUST SESSION
                  Stardust Tk 1
                  Stardust Tk 2
                  Stardust Tk 3
                  Stardust Tk 4 Master
EmArcy

6000              PRELUDE TO A KISS
                  They Can't Take That Away From Me
                  If I Knew Then
                  Prelude To A Kiss
                  You Hit The Spot

6001              IMAGES
                  Lover Man
                  Shulie A Bop
                  Polka Dots And Moonbeams
                  Body And Soul

6096              SARAH VAUGHAN
                  Jim
                  He's My Guy
                  -----------
                  -----------

6097              THE DIVINE SARAH
                  You're Not The Kind
                  April In Paris
                  ------------
                  ------------

6098              SARAH VAUGHAN SINCERELY
                  Embraceable You
                  I'm Glad There Is You
                  ---------------
                  ---------------

6099              SARAH VAUGHAN
                  Lullaby Of Birdland
                  September Song
                  -------------
                  -------------

6147              SARAH VAUGHAN
                  How High The Moon
                  I'll Never Smile Again
                  Over The Rainbow
                  Don't Be On The Outside

2-6163            title not known
(Double EP)       Lush Life
                  I'm The Girl
                  I've Got Some Crying To Do
```

                              Lonely Woman
                              My Romance
                              I'm Afraid The Masquerade Is Over
                              A Sinner Kissed An Angel
                              Shake Down The Stars

MERCURY (E)

MB 3129 (E)   Polka Dots And Moonbeams
                        Shulie A Bop
MB 3162 (E)   Easy Come, Easy Go Lover
                        Saturday
MB 3180 (E)   Old Devil Moon
                        Make Yourself Comfortable
MB 3210 (E)   And This Is My Beloved
                        Waltzing Down The Aisle
MF 1082 (E)   Passing Strangers
                        Always
MT 123 (E)   Fabulous Character
                        The Other Woman
MT 139 (E)   I've Got A New Heartache
                        The Banana Boat Song
MT 151 (E)   Poor Butterfly
                        Whatever Lola Wants
MT 164 (E)   Passing Strangers
                        The Door Is Open
MT 176 (E)   Band Of Angels
                        Please Mr. Brown
MT 198 (E)   Bewitched
                        My Darling, My Darling
MT 212 (E)   Padre
                        Spin Little Bottle
MT 222 (E)   Too Much, Too Soon
                        What's So Bad About It
AMT 1010 (E)   Everything I Do
                        I Ain't Hurting
AMT 1020 (E)   Alexander's Ragtime Band
                        No Limit
AMT 1029 (E)   Are You Certain
                        Cool Baby
AMT 1044 (E)   Careless
                        Separate Ways
AMT 1057 (E)   Broken-Hearted Melody
                        Misty
AMT 1071 (E)   Smooth Operator
                        Passing Strangers
AMT 1080 (E)   Eternally
                        You're My Baby
AMT 1087 (E)   Don't Look At Me That Way
                        Sweet Affection
MPT 7525 (E)   Poor Butterfly
                        The Door Is Open

yep 9507 (E)   April In Paris
                        Jim

C 30092 (E)   Broken-Hearted Melody
                        Misty

```
EP-1-600 (E)        title not known
                    They Can't Take That Away From Me
                    You Hit The Spot
                    If I Knew Then
                    Prelude To A Kiss

ere 1550 (E)        SARAH SWINGS OUT
                    Sometimes I'm Happy
                    Cherokee
                    Don't Be On The Outside
                    How High The Moon

mep 9509 (E)        DAMNED YANKEES
  .                 Whatever Lola Wants
                    -------------------
                    -------------------
                    -------------------

mep 9510 (E)        HIT PARADE Vol.2
                    Mr. Lucky
                    ---------
                    ---------
                    ---------

mep 9511 (E)        SARAH VAUGHAN HIT PARADE
                    Whatever Lola Wants
                    The Banana Boat Song
                    Mr. Wonderful
                    C'est La Vie

mep 9514 (E)        SARAH VAUGHAN HIT PARADE Vol.2
                    Poor Butterfly
                    April Gave Me One More Day
                    All The Things You Are
                    September Song

mep 9525 (E)        YOUR CHOICE
                    Please Mr. Brown
                    ---------------
                    ---------------
                    ---------------

mep 9535 (E)        BEST OF IRVING BERLIN Vol.1
                    Alexander's Ragtime Band
                    Isn't It A Lovely Day
                    You Forgot To Remember
                    Now It Can Be Told

mep 9536 (E)        BEST OF IRVING BERLIN Vol.2
                    I've Got My Love To Keep Me Warm
                    You're Just In Love
                    All My Life
                    Cheek To Cheek

yep 9057 (E)        SARAH VAUGHAN
                    Jim
                    April In Paris
                    --------------
                    --------------
```

zep 10002 (E)   SARAH AND BILLY
                       Alexander's Ragtime Band
                       No Limit
                       Passing Strangers
                       The Door Is Open

zep 10011 (E)   SONGS FROM SARAH
                       Cool Baby
                       Are You Certain
                       Every Thing I Do
                       I Ain't Hurtin'

zep 10030 (E)   AFTER HOURS AT LONDON HOUSE
                       Like Someone In Love
                       Three Little Words
                       I'll String Along With You

zep 10041 (E)   SARAH WITH FEELING
                       Broken-Hearted Melody
                       Misty
                       The Midnight Sun Will Never Set
                       Gone With The Wind

zep 10054 (E)   SMOOTH SARAH
                       Smooth Operator
                       Maybe It's Because
                       'S Wonderful
                       It's Magic

zep 10087 (E)   LIVE FOR LOVE
(sez 19006)   Live For Love
                       I'll Close My Eyes
                       Love Me

zep 10101 (E)   NO COUNT SARAH
                       Doodlin'
                       Just One Of Those Things
                       Moonlight In Vermont
                       Stardust

zep 10108 (E)   BEST OF IRVING BERLIN
                       You're Just In Love
                       Cheek To Cheek
                       I've Got My Love To Keep Me Warm
                       Remember

zep 10115 (E)   NO COUNT BLUES
                       Darn That Dream
                       Missing You
                       No Count Blues

zep 10121 (E)   MORE OF IRVING BERLIN
                       Isn't It A Lovely Day
                       Always
                       Easter Parade

10019 mce (E)   VAUGHAN WITH VOICES
                       My Coloring Book
                       Hey There

                    Deep Purple
                    The Days Of Wine And Roses

10020 mce (E)   VAUGHAN WITH VOICES Vol.2
                    Charade
                    It Could Happen To You
                    How Beautiful The Night
                    Blue Orchids

10025 mce (E)   PASSING STRANGERS
                    Passing Strangers
                    The Door Is Open
                    Remember
                    Always

10027 mce (E)   TOGETHER AGAIN
                    Bluesette
                    Isn't It A Lovely Day
                    You're Just In Love

10032 mce (E)   VIVA VAUGHAN
                    The Boy From Ipenama
                    Fascinating Rhythm
                    The Moment Of Truth
                    Quiet Nights

MGM

10549   Once In A While
                    The Man I Love
10592   The Lord's Prayer
                    Sometimes I Feel Like Motherless Child
10690   Dedicated To You
                    You're All I Need
10705   Tenderly
                    I'll Wait And Pray
10762   I Can't Get Started
                    What A Diff'rence A Day Made
10819   I Cover The Waterfront
                    Don't Worry 'Bout Me
10890   Im Thru With Love
                    I'm Gonna Sit Right Down And Write Myself
                      A Letter
11068   If You Could See Me Now
                    Don't Blame Me
11144   I Love You
                    Everyday

                    SARAH VAUGHAN SINGS
30339) part of   I've Got A Crush On You
      (album   My Kinda Love
30340) set   Body And Soul
      (No 71   You're Not The Kind
30341) (78s)   Ghost Of A Chance
      (K-71   I Can Make You Love Me
30342) (45s)   A Hundred Years From Today
      (---   You're Blase

```
                           TENDERLY
30730 ) part of     Tenderly
      ( album        If You Could See Me Now
30731 ) set          Don't Blame Me
      ( No 165       I'm Thru With Love
30732 ) (78s)        Once In A While
      ( K-165        I Cover The Waterfront
30733 ) (45s)        The Man I Love
      ( ---          Don't Worry 'Bout Me


X 1002              DEDICATED TO YOU
                    Dedicated To You
                    You're All I Need
                    Everyday
                    I Love You


X 1019              I'VE GOT A CRUSH ON YOU
                    I've Got A Crush On You
                    Don't Blame Me
                    What A Diff'rence A Day Made
                    I Can't Get Started


X 1020              THE MAN I LOVE
                    I Can Make You Love Me
                    Body And Soul
                    The Man I Love
                    Once In A While


MGM (E)

308                 Dedicated To You
                    You're All I Need
331                 I'll Wait And Pray
                    Tenderly
338                 I'm Gonna Sit Right Down And Write Myself
                       A Letter
                    I'm Thru With Love


MGM ep 538 (E)      SINGS AFTER DARK
                    Once In A While
                    The Man I Love
                    Don't Blame Me
                    I Cover The Waterfront


MGM ep 561 (E)      DEDICATED TO YOU
                    Dedicated To You
                    You're All I Need
                    Everyday
                    I Love You


MGM ep 572 (E)      SINGS AFTER DARK No 2
                    Tenderly
                    If You Could See Me Now
                    I'm Thru With Love
                    Don't Worry 'Bout Me


MGM ep 605 (E)      MY KINDA LOVE
                    Body And Soul
                    Ghost Of A Chance
```

```
                        I've Got A Crush On You
                        My Kinda Love

MGM ep 637 (E)          I'M THRU WITH LOVE
                        You're Blase
                        A Hundred Years From Today
                        You're Not The Kind
                        I'm Thru With Love

MGM ep 690              A ROOM WITH A VIEW
                        I Can't Get Started
                        --------------------
                        What A Diff'rence A Day Made
                        ----------------------------
```

MUSICRAFT

```
337                     Time And Again
                        --------------
354                     Lover Man
                        ---------
380                     If You Could See Me Now
                        You're Not The Kind
394                     You're Blase
                        ------------
398                     I Could Make You Love Me
                        My Kinda Love
421                     Don't Worry 'Bout Me
                        --------------------
446                     September Song
                        --------------
462                     Time After Time
                        ---------------
492                     Body And Soul
                        -------------
498                     A Hundred Years From Today
                        You're Blase
499                     I'm Thru With Love
                        Everything I Have Is Yours
500                     September Song
                        Don't Worry 'Bout Me
503                     I Cover The Waterfront
                        Ghost Of A Chance
504                     Tenderly
                        Don't Blame Me
505                     I've Got A Crush On You
                        Penthouse Serenade
523                     The Lord's Prayer
                        Sometimes I Feel Like A Motherless Child
533                     I Feel So Smoochie
                        Trouble Is A Man
539                     Gentleman Friend
                        The One I Love
557                     It's You Or No-One
                        It's Magic
567                     I'm Glad There Is You
                        Nature Boy
586                     I'll Wait And Pray
                        I Get A Kick Out Of You
```

140   Sarah Vaughan

593	Button Up Your Overcoat
	I'm Glad There Is You
15072	A Hundred Years From Today

PARLOPHONE (E)

R 3073	Body And Soul
	Penthouse Serenade
R 3077	Loverman

R 3123	The One I Love
	Nature Boy
R 3130	Don't Blame Me
	What A Diff'rence A Day Made
R 3154	Ghost Of A Chance
	Sometimes I Feel Like A Motherless Child
R 3170	It's Magic
	It's You Or No-One
R 3235	Time After Time
	Don't Blame Me

PHILIPS (E)

PB 373 (E)	Blues Serenade
	Spring Will Be A Little Late This Year
PB 455 (E)	Summertime
	I Cried For you

BBE 12036 (E)	SARAH VAUGHAN
	Come Rain Or Come Shine
	Nice Work If You Can Get It
	The Nearness Of You
	Ooh, Watcha Doin' To Me

BBE 12092 (E)	THE INCOMPARABLE SARAH VAUGHAN
	Black Coffee
	You're Mine You
	I Cried For You
	You Taught Me To Love Again

BBE 12094 (E)	AS YOU DESIRE ME
	Linger Awhile
	Just Friends
	Summertime
	As You Desire Me

ROULETTE

4256	My Dear Little Sweetheart
	Oooh, What A Day
4273	If I Were A Bell
	Teach Me Tonight
4285	Let's
	Serenata
4325	True Believer
	What's The Use
4343	Them There Eyes
	Green Leaves Of Summer

4359	Oh, Lover
	April
4378	Untouchable
	Hills Of Asissi
4397	Great Day
	If Love Is Good To Me
4413	Mama, He Treats Your Daughter Mean
	One Mint Julep
4443	I Could Write A Book
	Fly Me To The Moon
4482	There'll Be Other Times
	Call Me Irresponsible
4497	Snowbound
	Once Upon A Summertime
4516	I Believe In You
	What'll I Do
4547	Only
	Wallflower Waltz
4604	A Taste Of Honey
	The Good Life
RBJ 5	My Favorite Things
	Ill Wind
RBJ 6	Wrap Your Troubles In Dreams
	I'm Gonna Laugh You Right Out Of My Life
GG-67	Serenata

REP 1003	Oooh, What A Day
	Star Eyes
	Moon Over Miami
	The More I See You
REP 1008	If I Were A Bell
	Teach Me Tonight

REP 1026	Let's
	Serenata
	When Your Lover Has Gone
	Wrap Your Troubles In Dreams
REP 1028	Ain't No Use
	Have You Met Miss Jones
	You Stepped Out Of A Dream
	Jump For Joy
SERP-1-328	I Remember You
	Oh, You Crazy Moon
	Snowbound
	Spring Can Really Hang You Up The Most

ROYALE

1592	Lover Man

1829	Lover Man

Reissues And Budget LPs

ACCORD

SN 7195   SIMPLY DIVINE
You Stepped Out Of A Dream / Hands Across
The Table / You've Changed / Have You Met
Miss Jones / My Ideal / When Your Lover Has
Gone / Sophisticated Lady / In A Sentimental
Mood / My Favorite Things //

ALAMAC

QRS 2415   BILLY ECKSTINE AND HIS ORCHESTRA
Mean To Me / Don't Blame Me //

ALLEGRO

1592   SARAH VAUGHAN
The One I Love Belongs To Somebody Else /
It's You Or No-One / Love Me Or Leave Me / A
Hundred Years From Today / Penthouse
Serenade / Everything I Have Is Yours /
Lover Man / I'm Thru With Love / Don't
Worry 'Bout Me / September Song / Gentleman
Friend / I Feel So Smoochie / Trouble Is A
Man / It's Magic //

3080   SARAH VAUGHAN SINGS
I'm Thru With Love / Don't Worry 'Bout Me /
September Song / Gentleman Friend / I Feel
So Smoochie / Trouble Is A Man / It's
Magic / The One I Love Belongs To Somebody
Else / It's You Or No-One / Love Me Or
Leave Me / A Hundred Years From Today /
Time After Time / Everything I Have Is
Yours / Lover Man //

3108   SARAH VAUGHAN CONCERT
Penthouse Serenade / You're Blase / Ghost
Of A Chance / Don't Blame Me / I Cover The
Waterfront / What A Diff'rence A Day Made /

Nature Boy / I'm Glad There Is You / Tenderly / Body And Soul / My Kinda Love / I Can Make You Love Me / Sometimes I Feel Like A Motherless Child / The Lord's Prayer //

ALLEGRO (E)

ALL 801 (E)   YOU'RE MINE YOU
As Roulette 52082

ALL 812 (E)   BASIE / VAUGHAN
As Roulette 52061 with "There Are Such Things" omitted

ALTO

AL 712   MISS SARAH LOIS VAUGHAN
Vanity / Mean To Me / Tenderly / Perdido / Once In A While / Once In A While / I Cried For You / Street Of Dreams / Perdido / I Ran All The Way Home / Time To Go / Body And Soul / Nice Work If You Can Get It / Everything I Have Is Yours / Summertime / Linger A While / East Of The Sun //

AUDIOLAB

AL 1549   BILLY ECKSTINE AND HIS ORCHESTRA
I'll Wait And Pray //
BELL

41   THE VOICE OF SARAH VAUGHAN
The One I Love Belongs To Somebody Else / Love Me Or Leave Me / A Hundred Years From Today / Penthouse Serenade / Everything I Have Is Yours / I'm Thru With Love / Don't Worry 'Bout Me / September Song / I Feel So Smoochie / Trouble Is A Man //

BIRCHMOUNT

BM 687   GOLDEN HITS
Misty / Broken-Hearted Melody / Make Yourself Comfortable / Autumn In New York / Moonlight In Vermont / How Important Can It Be / Smooth Operator / Whatever Lola Wants / Lullaby Of Birdland / Eternally / Poor Butterfly / Close To You //

BOOK OF THE MONTH

10-5506
(boxed set)   SARAH VAUGHAN - AMERICAN SINGER
Little Girl Blue / But Not For Me / Autumn In New York / It Never Entered My Mind / Bewitched / Dancing In The Dark / The Man I Love / I'll Build A Stairway To Paradise / Isn't It A Pity / Of Thee I Sing / How Long Has This Been Going On / Lorelei / Smoke Gets In Your Eyes / Stardust / Darn That

Dream / Just One Of Those Things / Moonlight
In Vermont / Stormy Weather / I Cried For
You / You Go To My Head / Lover Man / Ain't
No Use / Wrap Your Trouble In Dreams / I
Want To Be Happy / All Alone / The Sweetest
Sounds / Every Day I Have The Blues / A
Foggy Day / My Funny Valentine / The
Nearness Of You / Watch What Happens //

BOULEVARD (E)

4103 (E)   WITH THE HOLLYWOOD ALLSTARS
Button Up Your Overcoat / I Can Make You
Love Me / Once In A While / I've Got A Crush
On You / Ghost Of A Chance / I'm Glad There
Is You / Nature Boy / It's You Or No-One /
It's Magic / The Lord's Prayer //

BULLDOG (E)

BD 1009 (E)   TENDERLY
Signing Off / East Of The Sun / Tenderly /
The Lord's Prayer / Sometimes I Feel Like A
Motherless Child / It's You Or No-One /
What A Diff'rence A Day Made / Gentleman
Friend / Time After Time / September Song /
A Hundred Years From Today / The One I Love
Belongs To Somebody Else //

CAMAY (E)

CA 3041 (E)   SASSY MEETS GEORGE SHEARING
You're Mine You / The Nearness Of You /
You're Not The Kind / These Things I Offer
You / Perdido //

CHARLIE PARKER RECORDS

CP 503   BIRD AT THE APOLLO
My Gentleman Friend / You're All I Need //

CHEVRON (E)

CHV 047 (E)   LEONARD FEATHER'S ENCYCLOPEDIA OF JAZZ Vol 1
Until I Met You //

CHV 082 (E)   DYNAMIC
You're Mine You / The Nearness Of You /
You're Not The Kind / These Things I Offer
You / Perdido / East Of The Sun / What More
Can A Woman Do / No Smoke Blues / I'd Rather
Have A Memory Than A Dream / Mean To Me //

CONCORD

3018   CONCERT
As Allegro 3018

CONTOUR (E)

6870 635 (E)   STAR PARADE
                  Sweet Georgia Brown //

6870 661 (E)   GIRLS,GIRLS,GIRLS
                  The Shadow Of Your Smile //

DEACON (E)

DEA 1020 (E)   BELTS THE HITS
                  As Chevron 082

EMBER (E)

EMB 3333 (E)   THE MANY MOODS OF SARAH VAUGHAN
                  Love Me Or Leave Me / Don't Worry 'Bout Me /
                  September Song / I'm Thru With Love / The
                  One I Love Belongs To Somebody Else /
                  Lover Man / I Feel So Smoochie / Trouble Is
                  A Man / My Gentleman Friend / A Hundred
                  Years From Today //

EMB 3335 (E)   TRIBUTE TO THE GRAND ORDER OF THE
                      WATER RATS
                  Don't Worry 'Bout Me //

EMB 3338 (E)   BILLY ECKSTINE AND HIS ORCHESTRA
                  I'll Wait And Pray //

EMB 3375 (E)   BACK TOGETHER
                  The More I See You / I'll Be Seeing You /
                  What Kind Of Fool Am I / Stormy Weather /
                  My Favorite Things / As Long As He Needs Me

EMB 3408 (E)   BACK TO BACK
                  East Of The Sun / What More Can A Woman Do /
                  No Smoke Blues / Mean To Me / Signing Off //

2012 (E)   SINGS
                  As Ember 3333

SE 8000 (E)   STAR EXPLOSION
                  Maria //

EMUS

ES 12007   DREAMY
                  As Roulette R 52046 with "You've Changed"
                  and "Moon Over Miami" omitted

ES 12009   DIVINE ONE
                  As Roulette 52060

ES 12010   WITH COUNT BASIE
                  As Roulette 52061

ES 12015   WE THREE
                  As Roulette 52108 with "Only" omitted

ES 12025   AFTER HOURS
                    As Roulette 52070

EROS (E)

8074 (E)   SARAH VAUGHAN AND COUNT BASIE
                    As Roulette 52061

8098 (E)   SARAH VAUGHAN - BILLY ECKSTINE
                    The More I See You / Stormy Weather / As
                    Long As He Needs Me / Maria / Fly Me To The
                    Moon / What Kind Of Fool Am I //

EVEREST ART FOLK

FS 250   SARAH VAUGHAN
                    I'm Thru' With Love / Everything I Have Is
                    Yours / Body And Soul / Penthouse Serenade /
                    Don't Worry 'Bout Me / My Kinda Love / If
                    You Could See Me Now / You're Not The Kind /
                    Lover Man / Nature Boy //

FS 271   SARAH VAUGHAN Vol.2
                    It's You Or No-One / Tenderly / The Lord's
                    Prayer / What A Diff'rence A Day Made / My
                    Gentleman Friend / Sometimes I Feel Like A
                    Motherless Child / The One I Love Belongs To
                    Somebody Else / September Song / Time After
                    Time / A Hundred Years From Today //

FS 325   SARAH VAUGHAN Vol.3
                    Love Me Or Leave Me / I Feel So Smoochie /
                    Trouble Is A Man / I Cover The Waterfront /
                    I Can Make You Love Me / I've Got A Crush On
                    You / I'll Wait And Pray / Button Up Your
                    Overcoat / I Get A Kick Out Of You / Don't
                    Blame Me //

FONTANA (E)

FJL 129 (E)   SASSY
                    As Mercury MG 20441

SFJL 9963 (E)   WHO IS THIS GIRL CALLED SASSY?
                    As Mercury MG 20831

FORUM / FORUM CIRCLE

9034   DREAMY
                    As Roulette 52046

9056   LULLABIES OF BIRDLAND
                    Perdido //

5067   THE MOST Vol 2
                    Moon Over Miami / Trees //

FCS 9085   SARAH VAUGHAN, JOE WILLIAMS AND BILLY
                        ECKSTINE
                        Hands Across The Table / I'll Be Seeing
                        You / My Ideal / Moon Over Miami //

GUESTAR

G-1418   SWINGIN' AND SINGIN'
                        I'll Wait And Pray //

G-1491   SARAH VAUGHAN AND MARTHA DILLARD
                        I'll Wait And Pray / It Might As Well Be
                        Spring / I'm Scared / You Go To My Head /
                        I Can Make You Love Me //

HARLEM HIT PARADE

HHP 8003   BROKEN-HEARTED MELODY
                        Broken-Hearted Melody / My Funny Valentine /
                        It's Delovely / Misty / If I Loved You /
                        I've Got The World On A String / Day By
                        Day / That's All / For All We Know / I'm
                        Afraid The Masquerade Is Over //

HI-FLY (Sw)

H-01 (Sz)   DIZZY GILLESPIE '46 LIVE AT THE SPOTLITE
                        Don't Blame Me

HI-LIFE

41   THE VOICE OF SARAH VAUGHAN
                        As Bell 41

IAJRC

20   STARS OF A MODERN JAZZ CONCERT
                        Once In A While / Mean To Me //

IL GIGANTI DEL JAZZ (It)

2 (It)   SARAH VAUGHAN
                        As Eurojazz EJ 1002

22 (It)   SARAH VAUGHAN
                        As Eurojazz EJ 1019

JAZZ ANTHROPOLOGY

JA 5164   RARE BROADCASTING PERFORMANCES
                        Everything I Have Is Yours //

KOALA

14107   THE LEGENDARY SARA AND BILLIE
                        East Of The Sun / Signing Off / No Smoke
                        Blues / What More Can A Woman Do / Mean
                        To Me //

LION

70052   SARAH VAUGHAN
I'm Gonna Sit Right Down And Write Myself A
Letter / What A Diff'rence A Day Made /
Tenderly / My Kinda Love / You're Not The
Kind / A Hundred Years From Today / I Can't
Get Started / I Can Make You Love Me / I've
Got A Crush On You / I'll Wait And Pray /
If You Could See Me Now / Don't Worry 'Bout
Me //

70088   BILLY AND SARAH
Dedicated To You / I Can't Get Started /
Ev'ry Day / What A Diff'rence A Day Made /
I Love You / A Hundred Years From Today /
You're All I Need / You're Not The Kind //

LONDON (E)

HBU 1049 (E)   WITH THE JOHN KIRBY ORCHESTRA
It Might As Well Be Spring / I Can Make You
Love Me / You Go to My Head / I'm Scared //

MASTERSEAL

MS 55   SARAH VAUGHAN SINGS SWEET AND SASSY
East Of The Sun / What More Can A Woman Do /
No Smoke Blues / I'd Rather Have A Memory
Than A Dream / Mean To Me / Interlude /
Signing Off //

MEMOIR (E)

MOIR 114 (E)   VAUGHAN AND VIOLINS
As Mercury MG 20370

MOIR 127 (E)   GREAT SONGS FROM HIT SHOWS
As Mercury MG 20244

METRO

539 S   TENDERLY
Tenderly / Don't Blame Me / A Hundred Years
From Today / I Can Make You Love Me / I'm
Thru With Love / Once In A While / My Kinda
Love / Don't Worry 'Bout Me / The Man I
Love / If You Could See Me Now //

MGM

E 165   TENDERLY
I'm Thru With Love / Don't Worry 'Bout Me /
I Cover The Waterfront / Tenderly / Don't
Blame Me / The Man I Love / One In A While /
If You Could See Me Now //

E 544   SINGS
I've Got A Crush On You / You're Blase / A

Hundred Years From Today / My Kinda Love /
Body And Soul / You're Not The Kind / I Can
Make You Love Me / Ghost Of A Chance //

E 3274 MY KINDA LOVE
Tenderly / If You Could See Me Now / Don't
Blame Me / I'm Thru With Love / Once In A
While / I Cover The Waterfront / The Man I
Love / Don't Worry 'Bout Me / Body And
Soul / I've Got A Crush On You / My Kinda
Love / Ghost Of A Chance //

MURRY HILL

927942 COLLECTORS HISTORY OF CLASSIC JAZZ
Body And Soul //

MUSICDISC

FV 372 SWEET AND SULTRY
As Masterseal MS 55

CV 120 title not known
As London HBU 1049

MUSIC FOR PLEASURE (E)

MFP 1107 (E) DIVINE ONE
As Roulette 52060

MFP 1130 (E) AFTER HOURS
As Roulette 52070

MFP 5233 (E) GREAT JAZZ SINGERS
Dedicated To You //

MUSIC ROOM SPECIAL

MRS 1006 SARAH VAUGHAN - DIZZY GILLESPIE
Love Me Or Leave Me / Body And Soul //

MRS 5024 SARAH VAUGHAN 1952
As Alto 712

MRS 5037 APOLLO CONCERTS 1950's
Street Of Dreams //

NAPOLEON

NLP 11091 title not known
I Get A Kick Out Of You //

ONYX

ORI 203 52ND STREET Vol 1
All Too Soon //

OZONE

17   WITH THE DIZZY GILLESPIE ORCHESTRA
                          Love Me Or Leave Me / Body And Soul //

PALACE

PST 673   SARAH VAUGHAN SWINGS OUT
                          East Of The Sun / Signing Off / No Smoke
                          Blues //

PARADE

SP 601   SINGS SWEET AND SASSY
                          As Masterseal MS 55

PHILIPS (E)

6636 224 (E)   NIGHT SONG
                          As Mercury MG 20941

6636 225 (E)   BLUE ORCHIDS
                          As Mercury MG 20882

6485 125 (E)   COPACABANA
                          As Pablo 2312 125

SONIC 031 (E)   SARAH VAUGHAN
                          Bill Bailey Won't You Please Come Home / I
                          Should Have Kissed Him More / Everyday I
                          Have The Blues / Sweet Georgia Brown / Lush
                          Life / Take The "A" Train / My Coloring
                          Book / S'posin / Happiness Is Just A Thing
                          Called Joe / Thou Swell / What Is This Thing
                          Called Love / September Song / I'm Just Wild
                          About Harry / Slow Hot Wind //

SONIC 037 (E)   PASSING STRANGERS
                          As Mercury SMCL 20155

PHOENIX

LP-2   THE SMALL GROUPS (1945-46) DIZZY GILLESPIE
                          Lover Man //

PICKWICK

PR 131   SINGS SONGS OF BROADWAY
                          As Hi-Life 41

number not   21 OF THE GREAT POP SONGS OF ALL TIME
  known   Body And Soul / September Song //

PLYMOUTH

12-115   SARAH VAUGHAN WITH DIZZY GILLESPIE AND
                            OTHER JAZZ STARS
                          East Of The Sun //

POLYDOR (E)

2344 049 (E)   52nd STREET Vol 1
                    All Too Soon //

PRESTIGE

PR 24030   IN THE BEGINNING
                    Lover Man //

PRESTO (E)

678 (E)   WITH THE CELEBRITIES
                    I Cover The Waterfront / Tenderly / Time
                    And Again / You're Blase / I Can't Get
                    Started / My Kinda Love / I You Could See
                    Me Now / What A Diff'rence A Day Made /
                    You're Not The Kind / Sometimes I Feel Like
                    A Motherless Child //

PYE (E)

GH 869 (E)   GOLDEN HOURS WITH COUNT BASIE
                    You Turned The Tables On Me / You Go To My
                    Head / The Gentleman Is A Dope / Lover Man /
                    Mean To Me / Perdido //

REMINGTON

RLP 1024   SARAH VAUGHAN WITH THE ALLSTAR BAND
                    HOT JAZZ
                    As Masterseal MS 55

RIVERSIDE

2511   WITH THE JOHN KIRBY ALLSTARS
                    As London HBU 1049

RONDOLETTE

35   SONGS OF BROADWAY
                    As Hi-Life 41

102   IN A PENSIVE MOOD
                    Sometimes I Feel Like A Motherless Child /
                    I'm Glad There Is You / Tenderly / Nature
                    Boy / The Lord's Prayer / It's Magic / It's
                    You Or No-One / Everything I Have Is Yours /
                    I'm Thru With Love / Don't Worry 'Bout Me /
                    Trouble Is A Man //

105   YEARS
                    titles not known

835   SINGS
                    titles not known

2-103   ECHOS
                    titles not known

RONDO

R 2005   INCOMPARABLE SARAH VAUGHAN,KETTY LESTER
                       AND MARGIE ANDERSON
                    It's Magic / I Feel So Smoochie / My
                    Gentleman Friend //

ROYALE

18149   SARAH VAUGHAN AND ORCHESTRA
                    Tenderly / Trouble Is A Man / Sometimes I
                    Feel Like A Motherless Child / The Lord's
                    Prayer //

SAGA (E)

6928 (E)   CHARLIE PARKER Vol 9. BIRD OF PARADISE
                    Lover Man //

Ero 8016 (E)   SASSY SINGS
                    As Presto 678 plus September Song / The One
                    I Love Belongs To Somebody Else //

8144 (E)   INIMITABLE
                    As Roulette 52060

Ero 8074 (E)   SARAH VAUGHAN - COUNT BASIE
                    As Roulette 52061

SCEPTER

CTN 18029   BEST OF SARAH VAUGHAN
                    You've Changed / Star Eyes / When Your Lover
                    Has Gone / I Remember You / I'm Scared /
                    You Go To My Head / When Sunny Gets Blue /
                    A Garden In The Rain / 'Round Midnight / It
                    Might As Well Be Spring / The Midnight Sun /
                    Stella By Starlight //

SMITHSONIAN

SCCJ-VIII/6   THE SMITHSONIAN COLLECTION OF CLASSIC JAZZ
(boxed set)   Dancing In The Dark / Ain't No Use //

SOCIETY (E)

SOC 981 (E)   THE FABULOUS SARAH VAUGHAN
                    I Can't Get Started / The Man I Love /
                    Tenderly / Don't Blame Me / How Am I To
                    Know / I Cover The Waterfront / Blue Grass /
                    I'm Gonna Sit Right Down And Write Myself A
                    Letter / Body And Soul / I Get A Kick Out Of
                    You //

SOC 987 (E)   WITH THE HOLLYWOOD ALLSTARS
                    Button Up Your Overcoat / I Can Make You
                    Love Me / Once In A While / I've Got A
                    Crush On You / Ghost Of A Chance / I'm Glad
                    There Is You / Nature Boy / It's You Or

                         No-One / It's Magic / The Lord's Prayer //

SOC 1001 (E)   SARH VAUGHAN , MEL TORME AND GEORGE CHAKIRIS
                     The Man I Love / I Can't Get Started //

SPINORAMA

S 73   SWEET , SULTRY AND SWINGIN'
                     As Masterseal MS 55

S 114   DIVINE SARAH AND MARGIE ANDERSON
                     You Go To My Head / It Might As Well Be
                     Spring / I Can Make You Love Me / I'm
                     Scared / We're Through //

SP5-601   SONGS FOR ANY SEASON
                     titles not known

SPOTLITE (E)

SPJ 100 (E)   TOGETHER WITH BILLY ECKSTINE
                     Mean To Me / Don't Blame Me //

108 (E)   ANTHROPOLOGY
                     Everything I Have Is Yours //

SPJ 150 D (E)   CHARLIE PARKER - EVERY BIT OF IT
                     What More Can A Woman Do / I'd Rather Have A
                     Memory Than A Dream / Mean To Me //

SRD

number not   GALAXY OF GOLDEN HITS
known   Broken-Hearted Melody //

SUTTON

289   title not known
                     Time After Time //

293   FEATURING THE VOICE OF SARAH VAUGHAN
                     I'm Gonna Sit Right Down And Write Myself A
                     Letter / Time After Time / You're Not The
                     Kind / Sometimes I Feel Like A Motherless
                     Child / The Lord's Prayer / I'll Wait And
                     Pray //

311   WITH PEARL BAILEY
                     titles not known

TIARA

TMT 7519 /   title not known
TST 519   My Kinda Love / The Lord's Prayer /
                     Sometimes I Feel Like A Motherless Child /
                     Love Me Or Leave Me / I'll Wait And Pray //

TOPLINE (E)

TOP 135 (E)   A FOGGY DAY
                     Thanks For The Memory / Start Believing Me
                     Now / My Funny Valentine / A Foggy Day /
                     Send In The Clowns / Like Someone In Love /
                     Detour Ahead / Three Little Words / I'll
                     String Along With You / If You Could See Me
                     Now //

TRANSATLANTIC

XTRA 1105   I'M THRU WITH LOVE
                     As Everest FS 250

CLDE 902   LOVERMAN
                     As Everest FS 250

TRIP

5501   WITH CLIFFORD BROWN
                     As EmArcy MG 36004

5517   SASSY WITH THE HAL MOONEY ORCHESTRA
                     As EmArcy MG 36089

5523   IN THE LAND OF HI-FI (WITH MILES DAVIS)
                     As EmArcy MG 36058

5551   SWINGIN' EASY
                     As EmArcy 36019

5562   NO COUNT SARAH
                     As Mercury MG 20441

5589   GREAT SONGS FROM HIT SHOWS
                     As Mercury 20244

5595   AFTER HOURS (LIVE AT LONDON HOUSE)
                     As Mercury MG 20383

VERNON

504   THAT EVERLOVIN' SASSY
                     I Can't Get Started / I'm Gonna Sit Right
                     Down And Write Myself A Letter / The Man I
                     Love / I'm Glad There Is You / Love Me Or
                     Leave Me / Ghost Of A Chance / My Kinda
                     Love / The Lord's Prayer //

VERVE

819 442-1   BILLY ECKSTINE EVERYTHING I HAVE IS YOURS
                        THE MGM YEARS
                     Ev'ry Day / I Love You / Dedicated To You /
                     You're All I Need / Passing Strangers //

V 8505   ESSENTIAL JAZZ VOCALS
                     Dedicated To You //

2352 171 (E)   THE VOCAL TOUCH
                      I've Got A Crush On You //

2354 041 (E)   THEY SOLD A MILLION Vol 2
                      title not known

VIKING

VKS 003   title not known
                      I Can Make You Love Me / Trouble Is A Man /
                      The One I Love Belongs To Somebody Else /
                      Button Up Your Overcoat //

VOGUE

CLVXR 600   GREAT JAZZ REUNION
                      Perdido //

SLVSXR 681   BIRDLAND ALLSTARS LIVE AT CARNEGIE HALL
                      As Roulette RE 126

VJD 534   SOUNDS OF SARAH VAUGHAN
                      Just In Time / When Sunny Gets Blue / All I
                      Do Is Dream Of You / I Understand /
                      Goodnight Sweetheart / Baby Won't You Please
                      Come Home / When Lights Are Low / Key
                      Largo / Just Squeeze Me / All Or Nothing At
                      All / The Very Thought Of You / I Believe
                      In You / Honeysuckle Rose / Moonlight On The
                      Ganges / The Lady's In Love With You / After
                      You've Gone / A Garden In The Rain / I Can't
                      Give You Anything But Love / The Trolley
                      Song / Im Gonna Live 'Till I Die / Falling
                      In Love With Love / Great Day / Nobody Else
                      But You //

WINDMILL (E)

WMD 135 (E)   LEONARD FEATHER'S ENCYCLOPEDIA OF JAZZ Vol 1
                      Until I Met You //

WMD 158 (E)   DYNAMIC
                      As Deacon 1020

WING

MGW 12123   ALLTIME FAVORITES
                      My Funny Valentine / If I Loved You / April
                      Gave Me One More Day / Saturday / Easy Come,
                      Easy Go Lover / Hit The Road To Dreamland /
                      It's DeLovely / Old Love / I've Got A New
                      Heartache / You'll Find Me There / Meet Me
                      Halfway //

SRW 16123   ALLTIME FAVORITES
                      As MGW 12123 with Hit The Road To Dreamland
                      and Meet Me Halfway omitted and The Bashful
                      Matador added.

MGW 12237   SASSY
                 Hey Naughty Papa / The Boy Next Door / Shake
                 Down The Stars / I'm Afraid The Masquerade
                 Is Over / Lush Life / A Sinner Kissed An
                 Angel / I've Got Some Crying To Do / Only
                 You Can Say / Cool Baby / For All We Know //

MGW 12280   MAGIC
                 As Mercury MG 20438 with Don't Look At Me
                 That Way and Love Is A Random Thing omitted

MGW 12360 /   VAUGHAN AND VIOLINS
SRW 16360   As Mercury MG 20370

WL 1083 (E)   COOL BABY
                 My Funny Valentine / Lush Life / It's
                 Delovely / Shake Down The Stars / Cool
                 Baby / I'm Afraid The Masquerade Is Over /
                 If I Loved You / A Sinner Kissed An Angel /
                 The Boy Next Door / For All We Know / Only
                 You Can Say / I've Got Some Crying To Do //

WORLD RECORD CLUB (E)

R 3 (E)   CONCERT
                 As Allegro 3018

R 15 (E)   GEORGIE AULD ORCHESTRA
                 A Hundred Years From Today //

TP 230 (E)   SINGS ALLTIME FAVORITES
                 As Wing SRW 16123

T 249 (E)   BILLY AND SARAH
                 Dedicated To You / I Can't Get Started /
                 Ev'ry Day / What A Diff'rence A Day Made /
                 I Love You / A Hundred Years From Today /
                 You're All I Need / You're Not The Kind //

WRC 440 (E)   DREAMY
                 As Roulette R 52046

TP 488 (E)   DIVINE ONE
                 As Roulette R 52060

ZIM

1002   BARRY ULANOV'S ALLSTAR METRONOME JAZZMEN
                 As Jazz Anthropology JA 5164

IV
INDEXES OF MUSICIANS
AND ORCHESTRAS

Musicians

Note:- Numbers Below Are Entry Numbers, Not Page Numbers.

Aarons, Al (tp) 11, 192, 193, 196.
Abato, Jimmy (sax) 40, 43 - 45, 47, 51, 57.
Adderley, Julian (as) 81, 82, 83.
Alexander, Bob (tb) 128.
Allen, Tracy (tb) 11.
Altpeter, L (tb) 52, 54.
Ammons, Gene (ts) 1, 3, 4.
Andre, Wayne (tb) 172, 175.
Angelo, Nelson (fender g) 205.
Arivoldo (perc) 205.
Auld, George (ts, lead) 2, 11, 13.

Bailey, Benny (tp) 217.
Bailey, Buster (cl) 8.
Bailey, Donald (d) 197.
Baird, Taswell (tb) 1, 3, 4.
Banzer, Russ (sax) 45, 47, 51, 52, 57.
Barker, William (d) 15.
Barone, Gary (tp) 193.
Barroso, Sergio (b) 205.
Basso, Gianni (sax) 217.
Batera, Chico (perc) 205.
Bauer, Billy (g) 20.
Baumartel, Thomas (fhr) 217.
Baxter, Joan (vcl) 217.
Beach, Frank (tp)
Beason, Bill (d) 8.
Bellson, Louis (d) 207.
Benjamin, Joe (b) 31, 49, 50, 53, 60, 65, 68, 71 - 74, 81 - 83.
Berg, Henning (tb) 217.
Berghoffer, Chuck (b) 193.
Bertrami, Claudio (b) 205.

Bertrami, Jose (fender p) 205.
Biviano, Lyn (tp) 206.
Blakey, Art (d) 1, 3, 4.
Blue, Danny (tp) 11.
Boden, Claus (ww) 217.
Bohanon, George (tb) 192.
Booker, Walter (b) 201 - 204.
Bossler, Andreas (ww) 217.
Boucaya, William (sax) 117.
Boyle, Dave (tb) 199 - 202.
Bradley, Will (tb) 32 - 34, 40, 45, 56.
Bredl, Otto (tb) 217.
Brereton, Clarence (tp) 8.
Bright, Ronnel (p) 113, 115, 117, 120, 121, 126 - 128, 130, 149.
Brockman, Gail (tp) 1, 3, 4.
Brown, Clifford (tp) 72, 73.
Brown, E (ww) 47.
Brown, Ray (b) 14, 193, 207.
Brown, Scoville (as) 16.
Bryce, Percy (d) 127, 130, 149.
Budwig, Monte (b) 196.
Bunker, Larry (vbs, perc) 193.
Butterfield, Billy (tp) 32, 34.
Byas, Don (ts) 6.
Byers, Billy (tb) 172 -174.
Byrnes, Bob (tb) 128.

Caiola, Al (g) 30, 34.
Cadavieco, Juan (perc) 173 - 175.
Carley, Dale (tp) 210.
Carney, Harry (reeds) 50.

Carroll, Frank (b) 37 - 40,
43 - 47, 51, 52, 54, 56, 57.
Carroll, John (tp) 37.
Casey, Al (g) 18, 21.
Catlett, Sid (d) 5.
Caymmi, Danilo (fl) 205.
Caymmi, Dorival (vcl) 205.
Caymmi, Dori (g) 219.
Chaloff, Serge (bar) 11, 13.
Chernet, Al (g) 128.
Childers, Buddy (tp) 192, 193.
Christlieb, Pete (sax) 193.
Gianecelli, John (b) 195.
Cincillo, P (tp) 57.
Clarke, Kenny (d) 12, 14, 23,
117.
Clayton, Buck (tp) 16.
Clayton, John (b) 206.
Clayton, PeeWee (g) 209.
Cleveland, Jimmy (tb) 173.
Cobb, Jimmy (d) 192, 195,
197, 201 -204.
Coe, Gene (tp) 192.
Coe, Tony (sax) 217.
Cohn, Al (ts) 11, 13.
Cohn, Sonny (tp) 131, 132,
206, 211.
Coker, Henry (tb), 68, 71,
74, 113, 115, 120, 121, 131,
132, 140 - 143.
Cole, Cozy (d) 18, 21, 34.
Cole, Nat King (vcl) 50.
Collins, John (g) 23.
Comfort, Joe (b) 152, 153.
Condoli, Conte (tp) 193.
Cook, Willie (tp) 50.
Cooper, Bob (ts) 193.
Cooper, Sid (as) 30, 32, 33.
Correa, William (perc) 174,
75.
Crawford, Jimmy (d) 10.
Cray, Gil (p) 199, 201,202.
Cullaz, Pierre (g) 117.
Culley, Wendell (tp) 68, 71,
74, 113, 115, 120, 121.
Cunningham, Ed (b) 11.
Cusamano, Bob (tp) 3, 7, 8.

Da Costa, Paulinho (perc)
219.
D'Agostino, John (tb) 25, 32,
33, 37, 54.
Das Neves, Wilson (d) 205,
210.
Datz, Mike (tb) 11, 13.
Davis, Eddie (ts) 14.
Davis, Miles (tp) 38, 39.

Davis, Richard (b) 95, 105 -
107, 113, 115, 117, 118,
120, 121, 126, 127, 130,
149.
Davis, Wild Bill (org) 53.
De Arango, Bill (g) 6.
Delmiro, Helio (g) 205, 210.
De Luca, Rude (tb) 11.
De Rosa, Vince (flgh) 193.
De Verteuil, Eddie (as, bar)
15.
Dixon, Eric (sax) 206, 211.
Dixon, Gus (tb) 13.
Dodge, John (sax) 199, 201,
202.
Domanico, Chuck (b) 219.
Donaldson, Bobby (d) 172 -
175.
Drelinger, Art (cl, ts) 30,
34, 35.
Duke, George (keyboards) 219.
Dupont, R (tb) 54.
Duvivier, George (b) 127,
145, 146, 174, 216.

Eckstine, Billy (vcl) 35,
99 - 101, 104.
Edison, Harry "Sweets" (tp)
127, 134, 135.
Edwards, Teddy (ts) 196.
Einhorn, Mauricio (harm) 205.
Elman, Ziggy (tp) 48.
Ericson, Rolf (tp) 217.
Estes, Alan (perc) 192.
Evans, Ken (vcl) 217.
Eyerman, Tim (sax) 199, 201,
202.

Farmer, Art (tp) 217.
Fatool, Nick (d) 48.
Faulise, Paul (tb) 173.
Feather, Leonard (p) 2.
Feld, Morey (d) 2.
Feldman, Harold (ts) 25, 32,
33, 51, 54, 57.
Ferretti, Andy (tp) 26, 32, 33
Fields, Kansas (d) 118.
Findley, Chuck (tp) 193.
Fishelson, Stan (tp) 41.
Fitzgerald, Ella 221.
Fleischer, Bernie (sax) 193.
Fletcher-Beach, Frank (tp) 48.
Foreman, Steve (perc) 200.
Foster, Frank (ts) 68, 71, 74,
113, 120, 121, 131, 153, 209
Fowkles, Charlie (bar) 68, 71,
74, 113, 120, 121, 131, 132,
140 - 143, 206.
Frazier, Bill (as) 1, 3, 4.

Orchestras

Note:- Numbers Below Are Entry Numbers, Not Page Numbers.

Bibliography And References

Atlantic Records Archives New York - Bob Porter
Barnes, Ken. SINATRA AND THE GREAT SONG STYLISTS. London,
England: Ian Allan Ltd, 1972.
BMG Music International Archives New York - Bernadette Moore.
Bruyninckx, Walter. SIXTY YEARS OF RECORDED JAZZ. Mechelen,
Belgium. Published Privately, Early 1970s.
CBS Columbia Record Archives New York - Martine McCarthy.
The Church of Jesus Christ of Later Day Saints Archives Salt
Lake City, Utah. Josephene Foulger.
Dance, Stanley. THE WORLD OF EARL HINES. New York: Charles
Scriber's Sons, 1977.
EMI - Roulette Archives London / New York - Michael Cuscuna.
GRAMOPHONE POPULAR RECORD CATALOGUE. Compiled by Edgar
Jackson. London: 1950s - 1960s.
JAZZ RECORDS 1942 - 1969. Edited by Jorgen Grunnet Jepsen,
Holte, Denmark: Karl Emil Knudsen. Early 1970s.
THE JOURNAL OF JAZZ DISCOGRAPHY. Edited and Published by
Chris Evans. Newport, Gwent: 1979.
Lees, Gene. SINGERS AND THE SONGS. New York: Oxford
University Press Inc, 1987.
McCarthy, Albert. Morgan, Alun. Oliver, Paul. Harrison, Max.
JAZZ ON RECORD. London: Hanover Books, 1968.
National Sound Archives The British Library - Paul Wilson.
Pablo Records Beverly Hills California - Norman Granz.
Polygram - Mercury - MGM Records Archives New Jersey -
Dennis Drake, Richard Seidel, Kiyoshi Koyama.
Schwann Long Playing Record Catalog New York.
Warner Brothers Records Archives California - Sheri Urban.
White, Mark. YOU MUST REMEMBER THIS. London: Fredrick Warne
(Publishers) Ltd, 1983.

About the Compiler

DENIS BROWN, an independent discographer in Birmingham, England, is developing a series on "The Great Vocalists," including Billy Eckstine, Vic Damone, Joe Williams, and Carmen McRae.